Dr. Richard Hayes – Adjunct Faculty | M
Theological Seminary Online

For many, the virtue of living life as a single adult may be difficult to pinpoint. There is a gnawing sense for many single adults that singleness is not a gift they possess, nor is that the true desire of their hearts. For many single adults finding a member of the opposite sex with which to share life remains a dream whether that be vocalized or repressed. The question remains then, how does a single adult with or without the gift of singleness navigate life and the Christian community solo. A former student, Kathleen Behrend offers a path forward for the adult single life. Singleness is a unique opportunity for Spiritual Formation. Drawing wisdom and practical insights from the Scripture, Kathleen draws a road map with the clear destination of the spiritual formation of the individual in mind. Readers of Behrend will find comfort, clarity and hope as they grow in the image and likeness of our Lord Jesus Christ in their character, conduct and outlook.

Darrell (and Priscilla) Derksen – Sr. Pastor | Enderby Chapel

"Marriage is a good dream. The Kingdom is a better one." Each page of Seeking Solo gives opportunity to explore the terrain of living single. It treats the subject with the utmost respect that it deserves and with a refreshing clarity. While not succumbing to offering simplified answers to those living the solo life it instead takes the reader on a journey to slowly explore the topic. It gives opportunity for God to speak to the heart, mind and soul. Seeking Solo asks the right questions and leads the reader who may feel like they are on a journey through a desert land to pools of living waters.

"Don't give your heart to someone who is not asking for it." A very honest conclusion drawn from her own deep introspection as one who is living Solo today. If you are looking for quick how too answers you will be disappointed. If your desire is for honest dialogue, it is a must read. There are books that consult God's Word to support the authors conclusions. In Seeking Solo you discover God's Word takes the lead. Kathleen leads you to know that you are worthy of the One who is Love.

While written for singles seeking more than our culture offers, the journey Seeking Solo takes the reader on is a welcome one. It draws you closer to God whom each of us has a deep desire to know. All are invited to come close not to a god of their making but to God who was has lovingly made us. I recommend the journey to you. I will recommend Seeking Solo to all in our church family. The 'all' is intentional as the journey Seeking Solo takes you on is a journey we all need to make.

Jori Dueck – Pastor | Emmanuel EFC

Seeking Solo is like sitting down with Kathleen in a cozy coffee shop as she shares her heart and story as a faithful Jesus follower in her singleness, encouraging you along in your own journey. She gracefully shares her disappointments and unmet dreams, while joyfully living in the gift of singleness. She openly shares her discouragements and struggles while seeking Jesus through it all and encourages us to do the same.

As a church, we have often failed at providing an inspiring vision of singleness. People are getting married much later in life. Divorce rates are as high as ever. More than ever before, people in our churches will tend to experience longer stretches of singleness in their lives. What does that look like? How do we not just suffer through it, but genuinely thrive and grow, taking advantage of the moment in which we find ourselves? The need for a thoughtful theological framework for singleness is paramount.

Kathleen honestly and vulnerable shares from her own experience. She finds her grounding in Scripture and builds upon other thinkers of the faith. She steps boldly and confidently into conversations from which the church has often shied away. And she does this all with warmth and encouragement, focusing on the goodness of God and the furthering of His Kingdom.

As you read, may you be encouraged as I was. May you see Jesus' love for you so clearly, and may you be inspired to seek first His Kingdom always.

SEEKING SOLO

A Journey

Toward a Healthy,

Biblical Season

of Singleness

KATHLEEN BEHREND

WESTBOW
PRESS*
A DIVISION OF THOMAS NELSON
& ZONDERVAN

WestBow Press books may be ordered through booksellers or by contacting:

WestBow Press
A Division of Thomas Nelson & Zondervan
1663 Liberty Drive
Bloomington, IN 47403
www.westbowpress.com
844-714-3454

ISBN: 979-8-3850-2942-6 (sc)
ISBN: 979-8-3850-2943-3 (e)

Library of Congress Control Number: 2024914398

Print information available on the last page.

WestBow Press rev. date: 07/30/2024

CONTENTS

||||||||||||||||||||||||||||||

ACKNOWLEDGEMENTS

God, this book is yours. You gave it to me, and I am honored and humbled to be the voice that you decided to use for this pathway. I literally owe you everything.

To all my friends and family who have patiently listened to me talking about the book I've been writing for the past five years; thank you.

To Mom and Dad, thank you for always having space for your daughter to come home and for all the wisdom through the ups and downs of singleness. I would not be the woman I am without y'all.

To Corrine Vooys, thank you for being my editor, mentor, and friend. Your editing elevated the content and helped me find clarity when I wanted to use Paul's run-on-sentences. And to think, it all began with a dress.

To Alex Gordon, ngā mihi i tō tautoko i a au. Your editorial suggestions helped me clarify the very first manuscript. I honestly reckon that the past nine years of friendship and conversations have shaped my thoughts in myriad ways. I'm sure you'll hear echoes of your voice in this book.

To Darrell, Priscilla, and Jori, thank you for your kind and encouraging words written for the forematter. To know that what I see in this book is easily perceived by others – without any prompting or explanation on my end – is confirmation of clear communication. Thank you for taking the time to read, offer feedback, and add your voice in speaking to the reader of the value herein.

To my Saturday 'morning' prayer crew; thank you to each one of you who encouraged me through this process, especially in prayerful support. Y'all are warriors and I'm thankful to have you on my crew!

To all my professors at Moody Bible Institute who spoke into this project, thank you for taking the time out of busy schedules to read the work of an aspiring author and encourage me to keep going.

To Dr. Richard Hayes, you went above and beyond. I am immensely grateful for our initial correspondence and your willingness to read multiple drafts of this manuscript. Your feedback helped me see gaps and tweaks that have made it 'more better' than what I could have done alone. Thank you for holding space to advise and for your patience with me through it all.

To Prof. Tami Stevenson, thank you for pushing me. "College Writing" could have been a class I coasted through, but you wrote me a note at the start which kept the fire burning. My writing evolved consistently via your instruction and attention. I so appreciate being seen and challenged in tandem.

To Dr. Rosalie de Rosset, I was not one of your official students and you still took the time to review a few chapters. Thank you for the feedback and for reminding me of some key truths that I had not adequately addressed.

To John Poysti, thank you for reading the first manuscript (nearly double the length of the book you now hold) in the space of days. I'm still blown away by your dedicated assistance to a Capernwray grad a decade after we met in Sweden. Your insight sparked the re-write and opened the door for the Holy Spirit to nudge me in a new direction.

To Eric Schroeder and the team at WestBow, thank you for giving the nudge to take the leap and for seeing this project through. It has become something more than it would have in my individual hands – yet again, "teamwork makes the dream work."

This list could be endless, so I have restrained myself to manuscript-specific appreciation.

My heart is overflowing with gratitude, cheers!.

PROLOGUE

IIIIIIIIIIIIIIIIIIIIIIIIIIIIIII

I wrote a book.

"Of course," you may be thinking, "I am reading the book you wrote."

No, my friend, not this book. I wrote a draft that came before, a book I needed to write to wrestle with truth and with my misconceptions about singleness. I am not entirely sure that I have gotten much further in destroying those lies since the many drafts of the first work. However, for whatever it is worth, I am writing this book again.

I have no intention of wowing you with a stunning twist of exegesis and hermeneutics, though I may have done a bit too much of that in round one. The Bible is important. It has a surprising amount to say about singleness; perhaps it is only surprising due to the lack of focus the topic receives from the pulpit. Not to lay the burden on the pastor, I do believe they should remember to speak into the season of singleness and not just focus on marriage, rather you should be growing in maturity and be able to chew on some spiritual meat that you find outside the messages of teaching pastors.

Each and every one of us who has chosen to follow Jesus has a responsibility to love God with the entire heart, soul, mind, and strength. Notice that your mind is on that list. I hope to engage your mind and your heart with this book, hopefully also your soul, and – highly unlikely – your strength. It may require some strength to continue reading difficult chapters, or at least to restrain yourself from tossing the book down and refusing to pick it back up. Otherwise, let us focus on the mind and heart. God can do plenty of work starting with those two.

In every effort to lay down the idol which marriage had become as the most fulfilling part of human existence, I tricked myself into thinking I actually wanted God more than a husband. Singleness is daily showing up to combat the lie that if I can manage to become content in my singleness, God will give me a husband. Healthy singleness is also simultaneously combating the lie that I am still single because I am not worthy of being chosen.

The goal of biblical singleness is spiritual formation; learning to live in congruence with Christ. I tried to make myself better as a person in an effort to force God's hand and fulfill my deepest longing for this earthly life; this is not congruence with Christ.

The season of singleness is good in its own right.

The length of it is not indicative of a lack of desirability or marriageable traits.

The length is not a punishment.

The length of my season of singleness is preparatory; it is a time to become the sort of person from whom marriage is about a Kingdom-focused partnership, for whom marriage is not a necessity to a happy life, and for whom marriage is about sharpening and giving and delighting in the otherness of others.

Many, if not most, of us will shy away from this level of deep introspection because we are not yet ready to face the answers and their consequences. Yet, it is one of the emotional gatekeepers to the narrow way; Jesus told those who followed him that if anyone would not pick up their cross daily and follow him, they could not be his disciples. Would not, an act of intentional will, becomes could not, an inability to follow Jesus. Part of picking up our cross is dying to the deep desires of self; this is true for every disciple of Jesus, single and married alike. Any desire of our heart that keeps us from following closely on the heels of Jesus will hold us back from the most beautiful expressions of singleness. It will stop you from being a true disciple.

BABY STEPS: LOVE IS...

Before we begin to explore singleness as spiritual formation, I have a foundational question for us to wrestle with. What does singleness teach me about the nature of love?

Here I want to turn to the famous passage on love, 1 Cor. 13:4-8, the same one we've all heard countless times during a wedding service. We've been so conditioned to think of this section in the context of marriage and vows that we tend to leave it in that space; it even has a place in meme culture. But Paul was speaking to the entire church community.

Love is a person, the trinitarian community that we recognize as the One true God. Lean in with me. There is so much wisdom in asking questions of Love.

"Love is *makrothymeō* [patient]" (13:4a); it does not seek to rush through a season, nor does it allow for hurry to be the pace of life. Patience is too soft an English word here to capture the richness of the Greek, *makrothymeō*. Thayer's Greek Lexicon tells us that the fuller definition is "to persevere patiently and bravely in enduring misfortunes and trials"[1]. This speaks deeply to me: how often does singleness feel like an ongoing misfortune and trial? It is a season I must face with perseverance if I want to develop in love. I need to be brave, knowing that it is not an easy season; while it is rich and beautiful, it is also very hard to trust God with an unfulfilled dream.

"Love is *chrēsteuomai* [kind]" (13:4b); it is not consumed with

1

bitter disappointment, especially when others receive the answer to prayer, and we are still waiting. Again, the Greek word has far more meaning than what we conceive as kindness; *chrēsteuomai* means to "show oneself useful, acting benevolently"[2]. Benevolence has fallen out of favor as a popular word in our current cultural moment, which is a shame. Kindness is a huge part, but it encompasses the quality of character that means well towards others. Singleness gives so many opportunities to develop in benevolence. A bitter person shaped by rejection cannot also be a person with the quality of kindness shaped by love. We need to allow love to uproot the bitterness that poisons our character so that we can move forwards in consistent kindness towards others.

"It does not *zēloō* [envy] (13:4c); here, Paul moves into the negative characteristics which cannot be defined as loving. Envy far too often colors my experience of singleness. Like *zēloō* reveals, "to have warmth of feeling for…earnestly covet, have desire, move with envy, be jealous over"[3], that warmth of feeling is a driving emotion of action. It pushes towards the object that inspires the feeling. In the season of singleness, envy relentlessly drives us towards the desired relationship that we see others experiencing. Love does the opposite. It is not forced to action because of unmet desire, especially when those around us have that desire being fulfilled.

"It does not boast, it is not proud" (13:4d); it is not full of itself, but rather is more concerned with others' wellbeing. This is not a call to put aside self-care. Your mental, physical, emotional, and spiritual health is important and only you can partner with the Spirit and tend to those areas of your being. However, this is a command to put aside the *absorption* with self. When your focus is fixated on your accomplishments, goals, dreams, and purposes, you will live in unhealthy relationships. Love does not promote itself.

"It does not dishonor others, is it not self-seeking" (13:5a); it does not compete for the affection and attention of a specific individual at the expense of another. Not that you cannot have close, intimate friendships which by nature exclude others but, rather, guard against interference rooted in jealousy. Relational sabotage is not fitting for followers of Jesus. Neither is flirtation for the sake of an emotional high, especially if there are suspected feelings; this is both dishonoring, disrespectful to the heart that has turned towards you, and self-seeking, thinking only about the fun to be had in receiving attention when you have no intention beyond entertainment.

"It is not easily *paroxynō* [angered]" (13:5c); *paroxynō* means "to make sharp"[4]. Anger is a natural human emotion, however, quickly becoming sharp is not healthy. Things that are sharp are most often used for weapons, either for offense or defense. Someone who is easily provoked to one or the other is not grounded in love.

"It keeps no record of *kakos* [wrongs]" (13:5d); it is not keeping score. Relationships will always have places of miscommunication and brokenness. Love does not create a system to remember what has been done against it, rather it openly, constantly, forgives. The Greek word translated as "wrongs" has a fascinating level to it. *Kakos* means "of a bad nature; not such as it ought to be" and "morally of a mode of thinking, feeling, acting; base, wrong, wicked towards persons"[5]. The hurts done to you by others should not have been. They might have had a moral bent which was legitimately wicked, or perhaps just wrong. However, all these injuries need to be healed, not held.

"Love does not delight in *adikia* [evil] but rejoices with the *alētheia* [truth]" (13:6); it does not enjoy the misfortune of others that has come unjustly to them. *Adikia* is "injustice of a judge" but also "unrighteousness of heart and life"[6] and *alētheia* is "universally in what is true in any matter under consideration" and "subjectively the candor of mind which is free from affection, pretense, simulation, falsehood, deceit"[7].

"It always *stegō* [protects]" (13:7a); it provides a safe space free from gossip, broken trust in confidential information, backstabbing, and so forth. Love fights for the wholeness of others, which includes being a shield or a guard for friends working through a season of weakness. The Greek reveals that this is ongoing: *stegō* is "covering to keep off something which threatens, to bear up against, hold out against, and so to endure, bear, forbear"[8]. Whatever the length of time, we have more capacity as single individuals to cover our friends. This can be done through intercessory prayer, conversations, or even physical presence.

"Always trusts, always hopes" (13:7b); it does not push back against God's good plan and turn away when he doesn't bring about our dreams in our timing, nor does it give up on the dream of marriage when singleness has no end in sight. Often, we have difficulty trusting God with our good desire for marriage because he doesn't follow our timeline. What we don't realize, or we choose to forget, is that he knows the full picture; were he to have given me marriage at any of the points along my twenties when I persistently petitioned him to do so, it wouldn't have been his best. I can see this retrospectively now that I've hit my thirties. It is still difficult at times to trust that God's plan really is better than mine, but he has never broken my trust. My hope is secure in him.

"Always *hypomenō* [perseveres]" (13:7c); though he could have used the same word which we discussed earlier for patience, Paul uses a different word here. *Hypomenō* is "to remain, to tarry behind" and "to endure, bear bravely and calmly"[9]. How often do we feel left behind in singleness! What a struggle it is to remain when our heart aches for deep intimacy, companionship, and romance. But love endures, bearing singleness bravely and calmly.

"Love never *ekpiptō* [fails]" (13:8a); it does not abandon the mission but continues forward even in difficult circumstances. Fail is translated from *ekpiptō*, "to fall from a place which one cannot keep, fall from its position"[10]. We are positioned strategically in singleness. It does not always feel that way, however the time spent being single is given to us as a gift with intention. Love does

4

not fall from this position, either accidentally or intentionally, because it keeps its marching orders through the good times and the challenging ones.

These verses give us such a full, well-rounded, expansive, and challenging picture of the character of love. As followers of Jesus this is the goal: to be made daily into the image of Love. No one is exempt. The season of singleness is an excellent training ground. It is just you and Jesus, living in various communities, unconstrained by the schedule of a romantic partner.

Growing in love gives us the rich soil to flourish in contentment. It is a holistic transformation that removes the focus from self-pity, bitterness, jealous striving, pride, and so forth - no area of self is untouched when love is the goal. These characteristics are all toxic to contentment; no one can learn to be satisfied in any situation when their attention is drawn away from Jesus, from Love.

WILDERNESS AND LEANING INTO SOLITUDE

IIIIIIIIIIIIIIIIIIIIIIIIIIIIIIII

I am a passionate woman. I feel deeply, I dream vividly, and I develop emotional attachments quickly. Especially to men who seem to check the boxes on the list for Suitable Husband. And yet, the season of singleness is unbroken. To quote Mr. Collins, of *Pride and Prejudice* fame, "...in spite of your manifold attractions, it is by no means certain that another offer of marriage may ever be made you."[1] Unlike Elizabeth Bennett, however, I am not waiting for another offer; I am just waiting for it to happen at all.

It is not unusual to have experienced a major heartbreak in the young adult phase, but I must admit that the man who broke my heart wasn't even my boyfriend. Honestly, I hadn't clued in to my true feelings until after he said "thank you" when I told him I was interested. Han Solo no longer stands alone as offering the very unfortunate response of "I know" when Princess Leia told him she loved him.[2]

I was devastated. For the first time in my life, I had come across a man who appeared to check every box, even ones I didn't know I had. A follower of Jesus *and* a pastor. A musician *and* an artist. Tall, handsome, and outgoing, I was hooked from the moment we met. However, he was sending me mixed signals and I needed clarity. I made the mistake of offering my heart to a man who wasn't asking for it, long before I exposed my interest.

6

There was no guard on my heart. There wasn't a check on my imagination or the clarity in my mind that I had found *the one*.

Unfortunately, certainty and interest must be mutual.

My confidence in his attachment quickly crumbled. It became a pile of ash, a burnt-up dream, a withered tree that had once blossomed with hope for the future. My broken heart retreated from the vibrant land of fantasy into the wilderness of waiting.

The wilderness stretches on. Vast open swaths of desert land, where the scorching heat of lust beats down relentlessly and there is no well to drink from. Winding valleys drop out of sight into inky blackness, where the shadows of disappointment, heartbreak, and unfulfilled dreams clutch at my flagging hope. Occasionally a cliff rises above it all, offering perspective on the journey behind, but little can be seen of what lies ahead. It is a sheer drop on one side and a steep path to go forwards. The way is narrow. Each step forward is a little shaky.

The wilderness is a difficult place to flourish, yet it is a necessary space for growth. Without the stillness, without deep soul searching unhindered by the usual noise and distraction of life, the harsh areas of our heart will go unnoticed. There are wounds that require silence to surface. There are roots that lie deep under years of whitewash, layers of varnish to keep suspicion at bay; nothing to see here. Everything is fine. Except, not everything is fine.

In every heart there is a deep longing for total intimacy. In the perfection of Eden, Adam and Eve "were both naked and they felt no shame" (NIV Gen 2:25). This is not just a physical nakedness, though the text shows us they did not bother with clothing until after the Fall, but a spiritual and emotional nakedness. There was nothing to hide. No fear of a deep, dark secret being found out. No suspicion that if the other person *really* knew the full you, then rejection would come. No running from insecurities by creating elaborate smokescreens. Adam and Eve could simply be, and do so together.

Where do you find satisfaction for the longing to experience such unhindered intimacy? This is a question we all must face in each season of our lives. Here, now, you and I are single. There is no covenant of marriage to explore the depths of possibility for human intimacy, naked and unashamed. However, that doesn't take intimacy off the table. It just requires a different channel.

Ultimately, only God can fill the longing in our soul to be totally known and fully accepted. Even in the best Kingdom-focused marriages, intimacy stops short, falls apart, and fails to satisfy. The same goes for friendships and family relationships. You will never have perfect intimacy with another human during your life because each of us is learning what it means to identify with Christ's death and resurrection. We are all developing our ability to put to death the sin-nature that fights the Spirit of God and wreaks havoc in our interactions with others.

God is the originator of marriage. He observed Adam's need to not be alone and created Eve as a helper. Fun fact for my fellow nerds: the Hebrew word for "help" is a masculine noun transliterated ʿēzer and it is most often used as a descriptor for God's aid.[3] Knowing that word alongside its normal biblical usage changes the usual perspective of the purpose of Eve. Simply put, there were things that Adam would be unable to do without the support and aid of Eve, just as there were many times in the Bible that the nation of Israel would have been wrecked without the support and aid of God. I do not say this to cast shade on certain dreams being impossible for a single individual but to help direct the conversation around a more biblical view of being a woman.

Because God is the originator of marriage, he is also the originator of the dream of being married. Yet, I struggle with this simply because, while it is true, it is not guaranteed.

God designed marriage.

God designed my heart to long for total intimacy. He is not surprised that I dream of marriage, nor is he toying with my emotions by allowing that dream to coexist with a long season of singleness.

Yet, my life is not any less fulfilling if I never experience marriage during my lifetime. At least, I pray that this will be true by the grace of God. I am learning to trust the goodness of God in the space of deep disappointment of a long unfulfilled dream that originated with him.

It is in that disappointment where the unique wilderness of singleness lies.

This specific space is characterized by the inability to rejoice in the new relationships of others, regardless of their long-awaited success in dating, engagement, or marriage; by the bitterness of soul that has drunk deep the dregs of rejection and never healed from the poison consumed; by a constant evaluation of anyone as a potential life partner; and often also by a relentless sex drive. All, some, or even one of these characteristics may be present in a "singleness desert". Yet, the underlying plane that lurks beneath any of these symptoms is the unrelenting feeling of being alone.

Alone. In our current cultural moment, we dread being alone to the point where we rarely truly are. If nothing else, your phone is a constant link to excessive accessibility to others. Yet, there is an aloneness that must be sat with in singleness and handed over to God, because, in doing so, you will realize that you are not alone.

Indeed, if you do not deal with the pervasive sense of aloneness, it will continue to attack you, lurking around the corner of every friendship and romantic partner. There is no place for the human soul to retreat to when feeling alone except to God. Jesus is the deep well who has an endless supply of presence, the true living waters that your soul cries out for, and the only one who will always be available to you.

Loneliness is a different sensation than aloneness. To feel lonely is to sense the need for companionship and ache for it to be filled. To feel alone is to feel alienated from all sources of contact, beyond the point of not quite connecting. I suspect that if we stay long enough in a place of loneliness we begin to interpret it as being alone, which then becomes our lived and felt experience. Indeed, many studies have been conducted on the effects of social and emotional isolation. "Moreover, indicated Dunkel Schetter, the effects that belonging and especially close social relations have, are reflected on the person's physiology, emotions, cognitions, and behavior, and ultimately significantly affects one's health… Campos and Kim (2017) reiterated that point and asserted that relationships, and especially close ones, are the significant center of the human social involvement, and based on related research have observed that relationship quality and their longevity are of significant importance for our health."[4]

In his book *Spirit of Disciplines*, Dallas Willard devotes a whole chapter to digging deeper into the Nature of Life:

> Anything with life in it can flourish only if it abandons itself to what lies beyond it, eventually to be lost as a *separate* being, though continuing to live on in relation to others. Life is inner power to reach and live "beyond". Human life cannot flourish as God intended it to, in a divinely inspired and upheld corporate rule over this grand globe, if we see ourselves as "on our own"…Men and women have the option of living under God and among other human beings in a cooperative relationship that fulfills their nature and makes the corporate rule of the earth the natural expression of who they are.[5]

Notice his statement about communal living under God and with others; it is *only* when we are active in relationships that we can flourish. It is in community that we discover God's purpose for humanity. When we allow our loneliness during singleness to develop into emotional isolation, we choose to live counter to the way that God formed us as relational beings.

My friends, none of this is a sin. It is not damning to live in this desert. However, to stay here creates too much room to cut yourself off from relationships, with God and with others, and to develop into a lifestyle that is so far beyond the intentions of God – one that plays into the hands of the devil. The enemy wants you to believe that you are alone because a person who truly believes in their deep isolation is easy to manipulate, to distort, and to use as a tool of destruction.

On the flip side, while wrestling with the feelings of being alone and turning them over to God, you can discover the truth that the psalmist prayed: "Where can I go from your Spirit? Where can I flee from your presence? If I go up to the heavens, you are there; if I make my bed in the depths, you are there. If I rise on the wings of the dawn, if I settle on the far side of the sea, even there your hand will guide me, your right hand will hold me fast" (139:7-10).[6] It is through the process of meditation and lamentation, of learning trust and clinging to the truth found in the Bible, through honest exploration of the deep parts of our soul which we'd prefer to leave buried, that our hearts can learn how near Jesus is. We need the wilderness seasons to have the space and quiet to leave the hurry and frantic pace of modern life; otherwise, the toxic thoughts that have sprouted from lies will go unchecked, unobserved, into the soil of our hearts and become a crop of darkness.

There is a vast difference between living in social isolation and retreating from the hurry of normal life to recharge. The former will put you at risk for depression; the latter will create a margin so you can process life in a healthy manner. Choosing to distance yourself from the social, emotional, and physical connections you need will stunt your potential to flourish. The lone wolves of society may pride themselves on their independence, however, they are far more susceptible to the dangers and stressors of life.

A time of solitude and silence is meant to be a retreat so you can return to your community as a healthier self, having processed deep wounds with Jesus and allowed him to minister healing.

Jesus himself made time for silence and solitude in the wilderness. Throughout the Gospels, we discover Jesus frequently retreating to the *erēmos*, the "solitary, desolate, lonely, uninhabited"[7] places, so that he could spend time in prayer. If the Son of God needed time alone, away from the crowds and busyness of life so that he could be still with the Father, why would we try to avoid following his example?

I discovered such wisdom in this discipline in the work of Ruth Hayley Barton. She writes: "[t]he invitation to solitude and silence is just that. It is an invitation to enter more deeply into the intimacy of relationship with the One who waits just outside the noise and busyness of our lives. It is an invitation to communication and communion with the One who is always present even when our awareness has been dulled by distraction. It is an invitation to the adventure of spiritual transformation in the deepest places of our being, an adventure that will result in greater freedom and authenticity and surrender to God than we have yet experienced."[8]

When you find yourself entering a wilderness season in singleness, know that it is not a punishment. It is God inviting you to experience his presence in a deeper way. It is an opportunity to face the feelings of emotional and social isolation and discover that, while you dream of a romantic partner to share your life with and are waiting for the fulfillment, you are not alone. In fact, you are never alone. Jesus is your companion on the journey. He is always present in every season of life and the source of the deepest intimacy, whether you find a human marriage or not.

I have spent too long wandering around in the wilderness, not fully aware of the depth of God's grace and provision in it. Years flowed together to surpass a decade and beyond of dreaming, only to be denied again and again. It has taken me a long time to trust

God with my singleness and my hope for marriage, to the point of learning to trust him with it whether he fulfills it or not. For me, this is a daily decision. Today, will I respond to God from a position of trust, submitting to whatever good he gives me and any difficult, tragic, traumatic, or simply awful circumstances that he allows? Will I face another day without a husband, or even a romantic interest, and lean into the knowledge that though I am lonely in singleness, I am not alone? The invitation is to say yes to both questions with the expectation that God will come alongside my journey with increasing nearness.

Singleness in my life seems to have had a parallel storyline to that of the Pharisees of Jesus' day: they believed if the whole community of Israel could follow Torah perfectly for a whole day, then God would end their exile and return them to the promised land *where he lived with them*. I have held the belief that if I can get all the various areas of my life to line up then God will end my singleness and give me a husband. To put it bluntly, I have tried to manipulate God. Seeing that it in writing, I cringe at my broken understanding of the Father. Such a view is more in line with the way the ancient pagans approached their various deities: offerings were specifically designed to gain their gods' favor so that the receiving god would do what they wanted. That is not the God revealed in the Bible, the One who chose to align so closely with humanity that he came as Jesus, who understands all our weakness intimately and desires to journey with us to bring us to wholeness.

As I discovered the beauty of the season of singleness through allowing God to tenderly lead me in the wilderness, to wrestle with why I felt so deeply alone and respond to his invitation to experience intimacy with him as the answer to my soul's longing, I also came to recognize my hypocrisy. I cannot just say that God is my deepest desire when I want a husband more than Jesus. That creates cognitive dissonance, chaos resulting from living out of a lie rather than my actual beliefs. In the wilderness, God not only dealt with my misplaced affection and disordered desires, but he also taught me to realign my life around "the *Way*, the *Truth*, and the *Life*" (John 14:6, emphasis mine).

I have not understood singleness. I have simply approached it with the attitude of "what can I get and how can I fill this time to dull the lonely waiting for a dream to stop being denied and passed over?" This is far too narrow, too worldly and dishonoring to God. Through the years of wrestling with the concept I am learning that there are tensions to singleness just as there are to marriage. My journey towards a more whole and holistic approach to singleness only began when I stopped trying to manipulate God and instead learned to seek him, sit with his wisdom, and pick up my cross daily to follow him.

The quiet, lonely, solitude, desolate place of the *erēmos* is just the place to begin. Within the week after I experienced my devastating heartbreak, the Spirit whispered to my heart: maybe God needed to free my heart to lead me on a journey to discover his. I didn't want to hear those words. I didn't want my heart to be free, I wanted it to be chosen by the man of my dreams. Yet, I couldn't easily dismiss those words; they had the weight, the tenor, the quality of the words of Jesus, and they stirred something deep within my soul. They invited me to leave a place to darkness and bitter resignation to ongoing rejection, and to step into an unknown vista.

Those words are here for you too, my friend. Will you respond to God's invitation to stop focusing on the broken places of your heart and take the first step on the journey to wholeness of the abundant life that can only be found in Jesus? Say yes. I can say from my own beautiful and challenging experience that it is still worth the journey of unknown duration.

He's waiting patiently. The ball is in your court.

Practice

Before you flip the page and keep reading, take a moment to sit quietly with the Lord and ask a few questions:

1. What thoughts, sentences, or concepts resonated with you? Which ones irritated you? What ideas did you immediately want to reject? Your visceral, emotional responses are teachers of truth that your body knows, and your mind may not be willing to process. Don't run from the visceral response; pain is an indication that healing is needed.
2. Based on the above exercise, are there memories or emotions that you need to process? How do you sit with being alone in this season?
3. Brainstorm ways to lean into God's healing work in the wilderness. This can include learning a new prayer discipline, contemplation, meditation, and other classic Christian spiritual disciplines.
4. What step is God inviting you to take because of this exercise?

CONTENTMENT AND CONSTRAINT

||||||||||||||||||||||||||||||

When I am infatuated, I am constantly distracted. I find it hard to be present to the people who are physically around me because I am longing for communication with the man who has caught my attention. This became increasingly obvious to me the year I had my heart broken. I did not want to talk to anyone else if I had *his* attention. And when he was busy doing life, aka not constantly available to me via text, I was agitated. Digital silence felt like rejection. Rejection from men was a sensation I had been well versed in feeling. So, any notification that buzzed my phone led to a quick draw to check for his response.

It was a very unhealthy attachment. I was so desperate for affirmation in the form of digital attention, as long-distance made for infrequent hang outs, that I was not content with the friends who were around me. Honestly, I just wanted to be chosen and valued by this one man more than I wanted to admit that I was already chosen and valued by a beautiful group of loving friends. Beyond that, I was already chosen and valued by God. But I wanted a husband and earthly romance more than I wanted the delight of the King of kings.

Years later, I still struggle with choosing contentment in singleness. In this space, I have recognized that God is not holding out on me. I am holding out on God.

Contentment is a learned behavior, part of discipleship to

Jesus. It involves becoming the sort of person who does not need to hide behind the security of another's choosing me because of the knowledge that Christ has already chosen me. As a learned behavior, it is also a formational habit. Repeatedly, psychology recognizes the effect of habits on our character. To return to Dallas Willard, "spiritual growth and vitality stem from what we actually *do* with our lives, from the *habits* we form, and from the *character* that results"[1].

We need to nourish habits that support, encourage, and grow contentment. Otherwise, we will continue to fight for fulfillment in unhealthy ways. Rather than see the goodness of singleness from a place of settled gratitude, we will struggle to escape the pain of the season through hurry, distraction, numbing, pleasure, addiction, etc. I have seen the truth of this in my own life. When I foster gratitude for what I have during my singleness, I don't feel in a rush to move on; the desire for marriage is still present, yet it is no longer the driving force guiding my life. Alternatively, when I allow bitterness and discontent to spread in my heart, singleness feels like a prison that I need to escape from. I am more likely to engage in unhealthy attachments, trying to draw attention and affirmation from any man who gives me any amount of flirtation. There is also a strong pull towards escapism, spending more time in a fantasy world than in the present moment. Those habits breed further discontent and create a downward spiral.

Paul talks about this beautifully in his letter to the Philippians. After commending their generosity in sending him financial resources multiple times, he tells them it was unnecessary. He was being held in jail and had no way to make money to buy food. There were no rations for him from the government. If he did not receive support from family or friends, he would starve to death, hence his gratitude for their gift. And yet, he tells them he was not in need "for I have learned to be content whatever the circumstances" (Phil 4:11).

Whatever the circumstances. Paul had experienced so much suffering for the sake of the Gospel: he knew starvation, brutal beatings, imprisonment, and terrible misfortune, and yet he knew contentment. In all of it. Through intimacy with Jesus, Paul learned contentment. I marvel at this. I have experienced far less rejection than Paul ever did, so why is it so hard for me to choose contentment in singleness?

Quite frankly, I deny the sufficiency of Christ to meet me where I'm at with all that I need for this very moment. I honestly don't want to choose to learn contentment because I am afraid that if I do, God will leave my season of singleness unbroken. My reasoning is flawed; in my stubborn will to decide for my own life what is good and what is bad, I push away God, who actually knows true goodness and the truly bad choices. In my limited judgement, I reject God's good and gracious gifts in the present moment. *Even if* he calls me to walk in singleness for the rest of my life, can I honestly say it is bad when I know that *his* will is "good, pleasing and perfect" (Rom 12:2b)? The only reason that I'm afraid to say yes to singleness every day is because I don't yet fully trust God; I desire to be married, first and foremost, over whatever he may have for me.

Singleness is teaching me the tension of *now and not yet*. The tension of love never giving up hope and dreaming without expiration date. The tension of honoring another with my life without having that relationship to keep me accountable leads me back to apprenticeship to Jesus. I try to hurry through now so that I can find my heart's desire in marriage, without pausing to submit each moment to the Lordship of Jesus. Contentment is learned through submission to the wisdom and goodness of God in giving and allowing whatever comes into my life each day.

To borrow the phrase which became the title of John Mark Comer's book, contentment is learned in "the ruthless elimination of hurry". He writes: "[h]urry and love are incompatible. All my worst moments…are when I'm in a hurry – late for an appointment, behind on my unrealistic to-do list, trying to cram too much into my day. I ooze anger, tension, a critical nagging – the antitheses of love"[2].

To be formed in contentment, we must first admit our discontent. How can anyone move out of a place they will not recognize they are in? "I'm fine" is a dangerous form of self-deception if, in reality, I am not fine at all. No one takes their prescribed medication if they believe the doctor misdiagnosed their condition. My friend, let us be honest; there are many, *many*, days when I am not content with singleness, either my experiences as a single individual or the very fact that I am still single and in my thirties.

But we cannot set up camp in the acknowledgement alone. Discontentment is an impoverished place to live. It keeps us in a hurry and cuts us off from abiding in the love of Christ. Let us move on beyond admittance and not wallow in all the reasons why we will not allow God to be sufficient in this season of singleness.

The great Canadian psychologist Donald Hebb is paraphrased as saying, "cells that fire together wire together."[3] When we focus on discontentment, we grow that headspace. Likewise, when we focus on contentment, we grow in contentment. It is not worth choosing to be a victim of discontent when the door to freedom is wide open; you begin your escape by recognizing the stronghold. Then you must take responsibility for your conscious thoughts and refuse to continue to perpetrate the cycle. It will take time, but, like Paul, you and I can learn to be content in all things.

What does contentment have to do with constraint? Essentially, constraint enables contentment. Constraint is placing limits on yourself. If you are intentional about learning to be content, you will quickly discover that it comes with restraint – in lifestyle, in attention, even in your prayer life to name a few key areas. For those of us who have grown up in a culture driven by materialism and immediate gratification, it may take more work to unravel the pernicious lies which have nibbled away at your contentment and begin to build healthy boundaries.

Constraint is a conscious lifestyle decision to say no to the ways of the world and say yes to the ways of the Word. Advertisements are designed to teach you that unless you have 'x' you cannot have the happiness that is visually promised. The faster you buy 'x' the sooner your life will look like the photoshopped models'. But I have no hesitation assuming that you know how quickly the buzz of a new buy – even a new relationship – fades. Constant accumulation does not give us happiness. Simplicity is a spiritual discipline that recognizes that we don't need more stuff to be happy; we need more of Jesus. Stuff requires attention and care to maintain it, which essentially means that you are investing your time long-term with each purchase, even if that time is just finding a spot to put it, forget about it, and eventually purge it.

I use materialism as an example because it is low-hanging fruit in our current cultural moment. The value of constraint in your purchasing habits is easy to imagine. Now, expand that. Take a moment to imagine what your life could look like if you exercised constraint in your use of free time, your media habits, your dating boundaries, your eating habits, your career aspirations, your potentially narcissistic self-care routine, and so forth. Any activity absorbs time; every activity will someday be called into account by our Lord Jesus, to determine if it was a worthwhile investment of our time, energy, and emotions.

Socrates is remembered as having said "an unexamined life is not a life worth living." Dr. Stephen Covey takes this in a more helpful direction when he advises people to "begin with the end in mind." He writes, "Each part of your life – today's behavior, tomorrow's behavior, next week's behavior, next month's behavior – can be examined in the context of the whole, of what really matters most to you. By keeping that end clearly in mind, you can make certain that whatever you do on any particular day does not violate the criteria you have defined as supremely important, and that each day of your life contributes in a meaningful way to the vision you have of your life as a whole."[4] Throughout the chapter on Habit 2, Covey states alternative centers which people tend to live from, especially when they do not take the time to examine their lives and priorities; they are "family centeredness, money centeredness, work centeredness, possession centeredness, pleasure centeredness, friend/enemy centeredness, church centeredness, and self-centeredness."[5]

In and of themselves, these subheading areas titled as alternative centers are not wrong. They simply cannot stand as central, especially not for an apprentice of Jesus. He needs to be your center, the One from which all other activity flows. Constraint as a spiritual discipline allows you to learn the necessary boundaries under the leadership of Jesus, to be led forward into true contentment.

Constraint is a combination of the fruit of the Sprit – patience and self-control especially – which means that we cannot force it to grow of our own volition. We need to receive the active grace of God flowing through our lives to build more constraint while simultaneously creating space for intentionally staying in connection with that grace. After all, Jesus is the vine and you are the branch; if you do not stay in close relationship, keeping in step with Jesus, you effectively cut yourself off from his living presence to flow through you. You cannot bear fruit alone (John 15:1-17). The boundaries that Jesus gave to his disciples are meant to help you and me bring more of the presence of God into the world; we actively join him and allow his life-giving presence to flow through us when we take constraint seriously.

We try to grasp and take what looks good to us as quickly as we can, because we are afraid. Afraid you will not have another opportunity; afraid God will not give you what you want; afraid you will miss out on all the pleasure the Western lifestyle has to offer. But this is simply a reiteration of the original temptation. "Did God really say..." is a refrain that continues to haunt and test each human being. As you learn to exercise constraint and stay within the good boundaries that God has set for your season of singleness, you will learn to be content with Paul and countless Christians who have walked this path before you.

To return to Comer, to the thesis that hurry destroys contentment, he discusses what Jesus offers us. Christ didn't come to give us an escape from a broken way of being, like the narrative of materialistic salvation the culture offers us, but he holds out equipment towards us. "He offers his apprentices a whole new way to bear the weight of our humanity: with ease. At his side. Like two oxen in a field, tied shoulder to shoulder. With Jesus doing all the heavy lifting. At his pace. Slow, unhurried, present to the moment, full of love and joy and peace."[5]

Slow, unhurried, present to the moment; that did not describe my journey of unhealthy attachment. I was rushing to get to engage in conversation again with the man of my dreams, instead of enjoying the people who were immediately present. I lost out on so many beautiful moments, deep enjoyment, and fellowship, because I wouldn't step back and choose to break the cycles of hurry that I had programmed into my heart. When I slow down, I can be present and really see people who need me now. It might be something as small as a hug and word of encouragement to brighten their mediocre day, and it might be a huge, heart-shifting conversation for which they need a safe processing space. Love sees those needs and responds in ways that lift others up. Love does not rush, pushing past others to get to whatever shiny goal is calling for its attention. Love is here and now. It is fully engaged, deeply involved, willing to lay itself down to serve others, and not self-absorbed in what it might be missing out on because it chose simply to be *here*.

I am learning the way of love and contentment in tandem. It is a challenging path because it goes against the grain of our current cultural moment. Love is an action, not a feeling; though there are pleasant feelings that come alongside, they are not the goal. Contentment fights on the battleground of materialism, pleasure-seeking, escapism, and general dissatisfaction with current circumstances. Empowered by the love of God, I can step away from the marketing algorithms that are trying to sell me a happy lifestyle by purchasing material goods. I can rejoice in my singleness when every romantic comedy tells me to do otherwise, when my friends are going on dates, getting married and having babies, when the nights are lonely and no one is available to just be present, when my schedule is crammed and I have no time to cook, when I just want someone to hold me, when my sex drive is on high and I still have no outlet. In all these things and more, I am learning to be content because I am also discovering the love of Jesus.

The journey is open to everyone. The invitation is here for you too.

Practice

Before you flip the page and keep reading, take a moment to sit quietly with the Lord and ask a few questions:

1. What thoughts, sentences, or concepts resonated with you? Which ones irritated you? What ideas did you immediately want to reject? Your visceral, emotional responses are teachers of truth that your body knows, and your mind may not be willing to process. Don't run from the visceral response; pain is an indication that healing is needed.

2. Based on the above exercise, are there memories or emotions that you need to process? Have you chosen to be a victim of singleness and learned the patterns of chronic discontent in this area?

3. Brainstorm ways to practice gratitude and contentment in your daily life. Give some thought to areas where you need to choose constraint in order to follow Jesus more closely.

4. What step is God inviting you to take because of this exercise?

BOUNDARIES IN SEXUALITY

|||||||||||||||||||||||||||||

It is 4:30am and I am awake.

I had been awake for some time; after a brief period of sleep, my brain had turned back on. All systems were fired up as the memory of the conversation pre-sleep returned to run circles in my circuits. Forbidden fruit, erotic desire, a healing balm to my willingly repressed sexuality and yet inflaming the lust lurking in my heart. By the world's standards, that description of the conversation is laughable as it contained little more than an attractive man offering to show me what kissing was like, if I was curious. Yet for me, who has so often questioned if I have any sexual appeal to men at all, it stoked a small ember quickly to flame.

In an effort to turn from the imaginative path I have too frequently trodden, I picked up the book I was reading, *The Making of Biblical Womanhood*, and was struck by this paragraph of Barr's:

> Women have always been wives and mothers, but it wasn't until the Protestant Reformation that being a wife and a mother became the "ideological touchstone of holiness" for women. Before the Reformation, women could gain spiritual authority by rejecting their sexuality. Virginity empowered them. Women became nuns and took religious

vows, and some, like Catherine of Siena and Hildegard of Bingen, found their voices rang with the authority of men. Indeed, the further removed medieval women were from the married state, the closer they were to God. After the Reformation, the opposite became true for Protestant women. The more closely they identified with being wives and mothers, the godlier they became.[1]

Since reading these words, especially that "women could gain spiritual authority by rejecting their sexuality; virginity empowered them," I have been wondering and praying. Am I really any closer to God because I have "rejected" my sexuality? Perhaps the answer is both yes and no, for I have only withheld it in physical action. My mental playground is another story and an area of constant repentance.

Now, it is very important to step aside here for a moment and address the elephant in the room. I am not advocating for the corrupt loopholes that sprang out of the vows of chastity taken by priests and nuns. The molestation and sexual abuse of children is a horrific part of church history that has continued into the current day, and it is inexcusable. My heart breaks for the ongoing impact of that twisted sexuality. There is a wide gulf between unhealthy sexuality because of repression and the conscientious choice to withhold sexual expression for a specific purpose.

That aside, it is amazing to me that I have made it thus far in life without 'defiling myself' with a man (to borrow the puritanical language). More than anything else, it is evidence of the immense grace of God. As all actions begin as thoughts, I wonder at how I have been sustained to step away from the lustful imaginations which have plagued me for far too long. I can only chalk it up to the work of the Spirit in self-control and preservation to limit the desires of the flesh.

Perhaps this is why I felt hesitant about last night's conversation.

Initially excited, buoyant to be seen as desirable to a man, it cooled to wondering if I even want to muddy the waters. I've made it this far and my life hasn't been devoid of pleasure because I have abstained from any level of sensual expression. What do I gain and what do I lose? I may never know if I continue on the current path of abstinence. However, strangely enough for a sleep deprived brain, the spark is cooled.

I'm more curious about the sexual ethic of the Kingdom of Jesus than about what it might be like to kiss a man. This is a surprising revelation.

Perhaps a fuller surrender is the key to unlocking something I have long been wondering. How do I channel my God-given *eros* if I follow the Kingdom ethic and never experience an earthly marriage? Can my virginity empower a deeper level of spiritual connection to God, as Barr shows was the example given by many exemplary medieval women? Is there another route to express sexuality, in social connection and creativity, outside of the physical realm of intercourse?

Eros. Most modern Westerners don't know quite what to do with this term. The Greek god of love, the root for erotic, and a term to encompass a wider realm of sexuality are all pieces that can be gathered under the umbrella.

In studying the dynamic between medical logos and medical eros, Morris gives a fantastic introduction to the broader concept:

> Even if we think of Eros merely as a figure who represents love—and no one seriously disputes the importance or complexities of love—Eros is much more than an ancient fictitious deity. As a classical god, Eros gives visible shape to the lowercase internal psychic force (eros) that has forged both a complex social history and far-reaching connections with other human forces, from lust and compassion to violence.

The classical god Eros, in this sense, bears some resemblance to fire...Like fire, eros can do great harm—burn, injure, devastate—but it also holds a primal power for good...Eros in its continual changes and ceaseless circulation, especially in what John Updike rightly calls its power to bind, once held absolute preeminence as the original cosmic creative force... Eros, in short, cannot be reduced to a concept. It is not accessible through propositions or argument. It is rather a primal force that, in its typical motion, sweeps us away, depriving us of reason, logic, and even coherent speech.[2]

We have all felt the primal force of eros. We have all been captivated by the creative energy, the deep urge to share of oneself in total intimacy and connect with others beyond the space of words. Some of us, like myself, seem to have an abundance of eros, while others are less enamored. It is part of our nature as humans made in the image of God, who was so full of love and creativity that he desired to have a broader community to share himself with. It is not eros that is our problem; it is how sin has twisted, mangled, amplified, and disordered both the desire and how we manifest and channel it.

Eros is more than sexuality. However, sexuality has become the major focus of this primal power in our current cultural moment. A cursory glance at most advertising schemes shows this to be so. Buy this watch, that perfume, come to this bar, purchase that ring, get these shoes, and so forth, with this promised result: have more sex. Some of the associations are abstract and some are borderline pornography, but the message is the same: order your life around your sexual expression; you deserve it.

Through the journey of singleness, I want to become the sort of person who is not ruled by the crushing weight of sexuality, which is not repressed but purposefully held back, in order to be under the reign of Love and not become a slave to dabbling in sexual experiences. My sexuality is not for sale. Deeper than sex-drive, I desire to learn to channel my eros properly in a way that honors God.

Part of this journey involves making peace with my body. There is still so much Platonic, and Cartesian, disconnect between our physical bodies and our invisible soul that is wreaking havoc in modern society. The biblical worldview shows that I *am* a body and I *am* a soul, not that I *have* a body in which I *have* a soul.[3] There are more recent discoveries in the scientific community that are confirming what our ancient spiritual ancestors already knew; there is more to our body than simply being a disposable tent to hold an immortal soul:

"[C]ontemporary psychologists and neuroscientists offer empirical evidence that 'the body thinks', arguing that what they refer to as 'embodied cognition' may be non-conscious rather than conscious, but can nevertheless influence conscious action as well as initiating thought (Cuddy-Keane). The neuroscientific discipline more closely concerned with narrative, the 'Philosophy of Mind', has introduced the term "embodied narrative" to refer to another aspect of the connection between body and mind: The narrative self."[4]

The Platonic/Cartesian disconnect does not lead to holistic discipleship. To keep my physical body as a separate entity will only lead to unhealthy obsessions with either caring too much or too little about it; the spectrum swings from abuse of the body because it is a temporary thing that will burn when the earth does to total indulgence of the body's every whim and fancy. Likewise, to keep my invisible soul as a separate entity will lead to a deeply privatized and individual spirituality, opposite of the will of God for the building, care and function of his church.

I suspect that we all know deep down that "there is more to us than meets the eye". Yet, what is visible as part of the outside, the physical world, is no less part of us. We express inner realities through external choices. From fashion to lifestyle, vocation to sexual exploration, the physical expression that others can observe tells them something about us. In the current selfie culture, painstakingly editing our virtual lives to reflect a heavily curated viewpoint into a controlled presentation of lifestyle, it is rarely an honest façade. More often than not, it is merely a projection of how we want others to see us instead of facing potential rejection if we were to expose our true self. Sadly, rather than celebrate the uniqueness of God's good creation, we conform to popular opinion and force our body to meet the shifting social expectation.

Friends, you are "fearfully and wonderfully made" (Ps 139:14). God did not make you poorly, mistakenly, cruelly, wrongly, broken, or any other harsh adjective you would like to accuse the Maker of. I've been there. I still struggle with aspects of my body, from living with an incurable chronic pain disorder to simply feeling generally unattractive according to the photoshopped beauty standards. God did not make a mistake when he created my body and my soul as a unique package, which inherently belong together. My body is not some random combination of DNA, family of origin, and historical placement that just happens to house my particular soul; I was "knit together in my mother's womb…my frame was not hidden from [God] when I was made in the secret place, when I was woven together in the depths of the earth. [God's] eyes saw my unformed body; all the days ordained for me were written in [his] book before one of them came to be" (Ps 139:13,15-16). This is equally true of you.

Paula Gooder has written a wise book on integrating our spirituality with our body, recognizing that we are a whole person, not a separate body and soul that need to be worked on in their respective vacuums. Her words speak deeply to incorporation:

> Beautiful bodies are not characterized by appearance but by inner and outer integration.

One of the themes that emerges from Paul is that my body includes but does not end with 'my' physical body. The description 'body' reaches beyond just my physicality to that which meets, honours and expresses love to those I meet. My body is our body, woven together in relationship. What makes a beautiful body is integration. 'The body' is made up of a wide range of aspects: the physical; that which is directed towards human life; that which is directed towards God; thoughts and actions; the way in which we relate to others; the way others relate to us. A beautiful body is one which finds all these elements, and more, in perfect harmony.[5]

Part of what makes her work extraordinary is her reminder that as Christians, we are even more than a body-soul composite to form a complete individual; we are a bigger body, unified by belief, which is meant to shape how we interact with others in relationship.

Obviously, this includes our expressions of sexuality. The biblical sexual ethic, especially that of Jesus, is narrow and well defined. It is not difficult to understand. Sex is designed by God to be an experience of total unity, two bodies becoming one in a way that reaches the soul in its binding power, between one genetic man and one genetic woman within the covenant of marriage. When the Pharisees were testing Jesus on the topic of divorce, he gave them God's definition for flourishing human marriage; "At the beginning the Creator 'made them male and female', and said, 'For this reason a man will leave his father and mother and be united to his wife, and the two will become one flesh'[.] So they are no longer two, but one flesh. Therefore what God has joined together, let no one separate…Moses permitted you to divorce your wives because your hearts were hard. But it was not this way from the beginning" (Matt 19:4-8). This view is debated, even within the church, because *we don't like it*, not because it isn't true.

Our current cultural moment will tell you that sex is easy, and by that they mean sex is cheap. "This is what cheap sex hath wrought: men perceiving women (and women in turn perceiving themselves) as having diminished 'value'."[6] While Regenerus focuses on the shift of the male perception of the female's value, this unhealthy attitude is expressed just as commonly from the women's side. The easier it is to gratify sexual desires the less value sex has; worse, and deeper, the less the individual sees themselves as valuable. Never in the course of history have women received so little in return for sex. Due to their increasing agency, opportunity, and success, women do not depend as much on men for their livelihoods and can therefore more openly pursue sex for its own sake, if they are so inclined. "It is not as if women receive nothing in return for sex, but they are asking for less in return – sexual pleasure, attention, affirmation, or simply an evening's worth of drinks and dinner."[7]

"When there is a surplus of women, or a perceived surplus of women, the whole mating system tends to shift towards short-term dating. Marriages become unstable. Divorces increase. Men don't have to commit, so they pursue a short-term mating strategy. Men are making that shift, and women are forced to go along with it in order to mate at all."[8]

This trend with a surplus of women is especially noticeable in church congregations; every church I've attended had a noticeably higher population of females, especially in the Millennial generation I belong to. The female surplus may not link as clearly to the divorce rates in the Western church as it does in the broader culture, since unrealistic expectations from the idolization of marriage are a strong factor for Christian unions falling apart, however, it does account for part of the weirdness of dating.

I bring all this up to say three things. First, that the church needs to be having more healthy conversations about sexuality. As a body of believers, we need to be a safe space for people to talk about their eros, both their libido and their underlying creative force that drives expressions of intimacy and the deep sharing of self, without giving in to the shame culture that the abstinence-only movement fostered.[9] God created sex and delights in it. Go and read the entire book of Song of Solomon, without the anachronistic lens of its existing as analogy for Christ loving the church. The author was Hebraic and knew nothing about God's plan to build a new community under the Messiah's lordship, so we need to respect his design in writing about sexual expression in marriage. That book in the Old Testament needs an *R* rating for explicit sexual content.

I have had several friends ask me to help process struggles with their sex life from a deep theological standpoint because they "trusted I wouldn't make things awkward" or add to the shame they had experienced when they were honest with other leaders in their church. This breaks my heart. Jesus expects his body to be at work in setting people free from shame and to be a space that brings wholeness to the entirety of a believer's life. When people don't feel comfortable or safe with other apprentices of Jesus to talk about their sexuality, they will have those conversations with people shaped by the modern Western values of cheap and easy sex. There is nothing helpful about the sex values of society if someone is struggling to understand what role eros plays in Jesus-centered singleness.

Second, without a healthy understanding of how God made us, as a composite of both a physical body and invisible soul-spirit-mind, it is increasingly challenging to follow Jesus. Unlike many of the 'gospel' messages that have been popular in the Western church, the invitation is not simply to go to heaven when you die, thus reinforcing the Platonic divide between body and soul. Jesus invites us to shoulder our cross daily, die to the disordered desires of the flesh that break down our relationship with God and others, and to follow him. He desires to redeem our whole life, including our body and what we do with it here and now. Sitting with the truth that Jesus cares about my earthly body changes my relationship with it; that it was formed with intention, and that it isn't some disposable tent to be tossed. My body is so uniquely part of what it means to be human that I will one day have a *resurrection body* somehow informed by my current form. These thoughts feel radical to write because they were not communicated to me while growing up in a Christian environment. Yet the witness of the Spirit and some solid research is convincing me otherwise.

Bodies are important. This needs to be a deeper conversation in the broader church world; my prayer is that as we talk more, we will find greater unity among denominations. Understanding the amazing unity within a human body of so many pieces was the inspiration for Paul when he wrote about how the church is meant to function and flourish together.

So much of the cultural view of bodies appears to be focused on sex appeal. How radical would the church community be if we all lived out the truth that our bodies are the temple of the Lord and therefore have infinite value beyond who we can seduce to have sex with us? Our bodies make up the temple both individually *and* communally. Paul wrote that anyone who has sex with a prostitute is making Christ's body equally united in that act (1 Cor 6:15-17 PAR); you can expand that to say that any follower of Jesus who has cheap and easy sex with another human being is bringing their whole church community into the bedroom and sins "against their own body" (1 Cor 6:18). Considering the body of Christ as Paul did, we should have more serious conversations about casual sex within the church because it impacts the whole community, not just the members engaging in intercourse.

Third, our expression of eros will either grow us towards love or lust, in becoming children of light or of darkness. Sex outside of a marriage covenant ignores at least half of the fruit of the Spirit: love, patience, faithfulness, self-control, though it could be argued that kindness and goodness are also not in play with cheap sex.

This topic is probably another book in and of itself. However, it is worth mentioning that Jesus is grieved when his children are driven by lust instead of love.

From dehumanizing and dishonoring those that you think about as a body to satisfy a desire, to being ruled by your base impulses, when you are so controlled by your eros that you cannot imagine a lifestyle of singleness without sex, you show that you are more interested in worshiping Aphrodite – the ancient goddess of love, sex, and fertility – than Jesus. Boundaries to keep sexual expression for the covenant of marriage show that you are sexually free rather than repressed. Cheap and easy sex keeps you enslaved to a system which demands constant pleasure. As Dr. Leaf notes, "Chemicals are released and exchanged in the male and the female brains when they talk, kiss and touch. These chemicals interchange and react, and a chemical imprint forms in each other's brains... Because the brain is designed for one partner, confusion will arise when these same bonds are formed with multiple partners."[10]

Sadly, much of the message taught in the Western church is that sex is bad so do not do it, unless you are married, in which case go hard. This is certainly the message I grew up with through the nineties to early 2000's. Because I was just as curious as a pre-teen as I am now, I did my own searching. I was not content to be told that the Bible says sex is bad, I wanted to find out where it says that and why. So I read the Bible, finding no verse that specifically said what my church said, and books on dating, finding some bizarre boundaries alongside helpful ones. As far as I could discern as a child, unless you were married, all other sex was adultery; the person you slept with was someone's not-yet-spouse. Since Jesus was clear on adultery, and took it to the heart level of intent, my teenage brain had some sort of footing to understand the fuss around pre-marital sex.

Through ongoing study and curiosity, I have found that the Bible has a lot to say about sex and boundaries, often in indirect but very applicable ways. There are also enough key verses that are explicit, a handful I'll list here for you to explore: Matt 15:19, Acts 15:20, Rom 1:24, 1 Cor 6:13, 18, 1 Thess 4:3.

Most modern English translations of the New Testament use 'sexual immorality' for *porneia* because the old school 'fornication' or 'illicit sex' holds little meaning in our current cultural moment. The trouble with this translation choice is that it is so easy to skip over when we are indoctrinated by a societal mood that is pro-sex in any and every form. Very few people think of sex outside of marriage as immoral, especially as socio-cultural expectations are pushing against legislature. Constant shifting on what is defined as 'illicit sex' comes with each change of social mood. "American judges were not the first people to equate marriage and sexual licitness -this link had deep roots in Christian constructions of sexual morality that posited marriage as the site where lust was transformed into virtue." Dubler goes on to discuss how the "religious underpinnings" were not sufficient for legislature, especially as society expected the legal system to be separate from religion.[11] 'Immorality' is becoming archaic alongside 'fornication'. It might help to read 'cheap/easy sex' every time you come across 'sexual immorality' as a reminder that the sexual ethic of Jesus is firmly and clearly counter-cultural.

The way we view God influences our sexual expression. As Paul writes, "they neither glorified him as God nor gave thanks to him, but their thinking became futile and their foolish hearts were darkened...therefore God gave them over in the sinful desires of their hearts to sexual impurity for the degrading of their bodies with one another" (Rom 1:21, 24). To paraphrase it myself, when we refuse to accept God's design for human flourishing and disregard the ethics that he has woven into our very nature, we are easily misled to believe that boundary-less sexuality is the deepest, most gratifying experience of humanity. That path of cheap and easy sex leads to degradation of the body, both individually and corporately as the body of Christ. Yet, if we flip the passage to find the positive, choosing to let go of the desires in our heart for immediate sex to instead glorify God and give thanks to him, our thinking will become fruitful, and our hearts illuminated and wise.

To those who have crossed the boundary line that Jesus gave us and have willingly engaged in sexual activity, know that there is both forgiveness and grace available to you. You need not be burdened by shame for the choices made in this realm nor do you have anything less to offer in a marriage; the myth reimagined in the evangelical purity movement, that those who are virgins are more spiritually pure, has created havoc in the lives of countless individuals.[12] It is a myth, albeit one built upon God's design for healthy sexual expression. I can remember the metaphor of a rose being passed around in the church circles I grew up in; those who engaged in sex outside of marriage were flowers that had been crushed, their petals torn off, and were a pathetic thing to offer to a future spouse. It was not a healthy or helpful way to teach teenagers about Jesus' sexual ethic. Rather, it created bondage to shame, fear, guilt, or rebellion against the puritanical teachings.

Foremost, allow the peace of God to wash over you as you trust his forgiveness. It is wise to seek counselling to do the inner healing work so you can detach from any toxic thoughts that strangle your mind. Wrestle with understanding the boundaries that God has given us for healthy sexual expression; it is all right if you struggle with accepting the narrow way that Jesus taught. Please do not simply dismiss it as archaic and out of touch with reality. Jesus designed sex. He knows what he is talking about.

Create healthy boundaries. Pray constantly. Honestly acknowledge your struggles with following Jesus regarding your sexuality; God is not shocked or surprised by your desires, yet he also longs to give you freedom from lust. This harmful imaginative practice dehumanizes those you fantasize about and hardens your heart.

I want that wisdom for you. It is never too late to start living a life of constrained sexuality according to the Way of Jesus. May you know that there is no shame over any expressions of sexuality that you have chosen or that have been forced upon you; in the loving embrace of our Father there is sorrow and a desire for a turning to his understanding of sex, not a condemning command or a soul-crushing, shame-inducing rant. God gives sexual boundaries in his Word because he desires that you would live in sexual freedom through restraint, not sexual bondage through abuse of his design.

Practice

Before you flip the page and keep reading, take a moment to sit quietly with the Lord and ask a few questions:

1. What thoughts, sentences, or concepts resonated with you? Which ones irritated you? What ideas did you immediately want to reject? Your visceral, emotional responses are teachers of truth that your body knows, and your mind may not be willing to process. Don't run from the visceral response; pain is an indication that healing is needed.
2. Based on the above exercise, are there memories or emotions that you need to process? Do you need to confess areas of wayward sexuality to a counsellor or bring traumatic sexual exploitation into the light?
3. Take a moment to forgive yourself (and others) for misconduct in sexuality. We all need to practice extra grace here in the highly sexualized cultural moment.
4. What step is God inviting you to take because of this exercise?

FIND YOUR FELLOWSHIP

Looking back at my life, there are two major threads that intertwine deeply with contentment in singleness; the first is when I'm experiencing deep union with Jesus and nothing on earth seems to matter – a state of being that is infrequent for me – and the other is when I have healthy, deep, enriching friendships, preferably within a group that frequently gets together. I have said on more than one occasion, getting home after a fulfilling night of fellowship, that perhaps I really could do this singleness thing forever if God made it clear. Yet, even the best of friendships leaves something lacking, and I usually regret thinking I would survive lifelong singleness.

One such friendship that was a particularly dear season was the summer that I met Steph. Ironically, I nearly wrote her off as a friend because I was jealous that she had joined a youth group meeting *with* Adam, who I then had a crush on. It's painful to admit how shallow I can be sometimes. I had to force myself to overcome that unfair reaction and evaluate her simply as a fellow human being. To this day, we are both grateful I did because once we started hanging out, we immediately discovered we were kindred souls. That summer we were both job hunting, I had just finished a fashion internship with Roxanne Nikki, and Steph was picking up day calls in the acting world, so we were wildly available for adventures. Many afternoons I would bike to the half-sculpture-storage-half-loft where Steph was living and we would talk about what Jesus was doing in our lives and how he was leading us, or we would watch movies and cook together.

Steph knew about Adam. We talked in depth about my very honest and open chat with him regarding my feelings, getting past that rejection, and continuing to be his 'nerd sister'. Having her friendship was a crucial part of my healing journey; it is hard to be hung up on a crush when you are having so much fun with a kindred spirit. So, years later when he asked her out, I was free to be excited for her, even though she was still trying to understand her own feelings. Because of my prior interest, she never looked in Adam's direction until there he was, ready to pursue her. Side note: they just celebrated four years of marriage. There is something so incredible about standing up for two very dear friends committing their lives together in a stubborn, rugged covenant.

God knew that I needed Steph just as much as she needed me. Our first meeting was obviously shaky, but he would not let my jealousy ruin a beautiful friendship. Honestly, I could have stayed jealous. He would not have forced my hand. Yet, I also trust my intuition with people, so when a kindred spirit was present, there was no way I would let a crush ruin that. That one summer of frequent fellowship became the support structure that has held us together as long-distance sisters. We joke that the world can only handle the two of us in the same city for a short time; Steph went to YWAM Australia while I stayed in Vancouver and worked at a Starbucks, and shortly after she returned, I moved spontaneously to New Zealand. It didn't matter the time zone difference. Somehow, God lined up our free moments so that we were available for the other when we needed to process and pray.

The beauty, and pain, of friendships is that they are seasonal. Some are life-long; I can count mine on one hand. Others last weeks, months, years, or decades. You never know how long a friendship will last and what the parameters will be. I believe any time there is opportunity to pour into another human and develop a deep connection, it is worth it. Even if they are no longer a major part of your story after a short season, it is better to love generously than withhold friendship out of fear.

I have found that maintaining a seasonal view of friendship helps me deal with the grief that accompanies the ending. Gratitude for the memories made takes center stage, rather than bitterness over the loss of companionship. This does not take the pain away, but it does give a healthy framework for processing, especially if the friend drifts off; spectacular explosions and backstabbing betrayal require more intensive healing for forgiveness to take place.

God made humans for community. The first thing in the creation narrative that came with the label 'not good' was Adam working alone in the garden.[1] As you continue to read in Genesis 2, you will see that animals were not suitable companions in the place of another human being. Even the most intense introverts among my friends know they need human contact, no matter how much they love their cat or dog or books or games.

We are living in days of loneliness. The number of Americans who die from causes attributable to social isolation is higher than cancer or stroke. In 2018, the UK set up a Ministry of Loneliness to fight the challenges of modern society; there are serious links between social isolation and the growing opioid/suicide crisis.[2] "The absence of belonging is so widespread that we might say we are living in an age of isolation, imitating the lament from early in the last century, when life was referred to as the age of anxiety."[3]

Living well in the season of singleness needs deep and fulfilling fellowship. Personally, I reckon this should cross as many socio-cultural boundaries as possible. Make friends with those who are older, retired grandparents to parents with teenage or adult children, who have the capacity to give wisdom from their life experience. Spend time with those who are in your own generation, so that you can share experiences, life struggles, and support each other. Likewise, get to know those who are younger, by many years or few, so that you have others to support in seasons you have already walked through. Befriend those of other cultures, countries, denominations, religions, and gender. Interacting with people who hold different worldviews is important to learn skills for unity, conflict resolution and empathy - plus, it is fun to try to understand how others could think so radically unlike your own headspace.

Theoretically, this is how the general, local church should look, as a unified collective of every age, economic situation, gender, tribe, nation, and tongue, praising our Lord Jesus. However, I'm sure we all know homogenous churches where you couldn't throw a stone without hitting multiple hipsters in skinny jeans, or a dozen grumpy old white men, or a group of black gospel singers, or any other stereotype you'd like to add here. Like attracts like, who then find it easy to build fences to keep the outsiders out. This isn't the way of Jesus; he was constantly taking criticism for keeping company with all the sinners, people who couldn't be further from his pure and holy God-nature. His closest twelve disciples included a tax collector – despised for working for the Roman enemies and profiting by pocketing extra tax on their fellow Jews – and a Zealot – a member of a cult which harassed the Roman officers and took extra offense at Jews who sided with the oppressors. It is easy to imagine the tension at the dinner table. Yet, Matthew and Simon were able to work together to build the church after years of following Jesus in the same crew.

Entire books could be and have been written on the problem of unity, also known as the lack thereof, in the body of Christ. That is not the scope of this book or this chapter. I bring it up as a reminder to make friends with people outside of your general circle. It brings its own set of challenges, but so far, I've discovered it to always be worth the risk.

I want to continue to become someone who invests more in deep friendship than fleeting feelings. Crushes come and crushes go; occasionally, they continue as friends, of varying degrees for years after honest conversations. Yet, I have learned the hard way that it isn't healthy or helpful to fixate on growing a relationship with a man who is not interested. I have a little saying I tell myself when I notice that I'm falling into an old habit, born out of rejection and fear, and I go overboard to make myself a valuable part of his life: don't give your heart to someone who isn't asking for it.

A quick aside to my female friends; if a man is not putting in effort to make you a part of his life, he is simply not interested. I have had this confirmed by all my male friends. A man *will* make time with you if he *wants* to. Yes, there may be interest that he is holding back for a variety of reasons, but can we all just decide to take better care of our hearts and be patient with the men in our lives? I am not advocating playing hard to get. Mind games are a cruel form of social torture. Ladies, have a little respect for yourself: you *are* worth pursuing. This also does not mean that he must do all the work – reciprocation is a necessary part of any relationship – but it does mean that you should not force yourself into his life. If you need to have an honest conversation and get real about your feelings, be bold and do it. I have found it necessary for healing my heart just to know that a door is fully shut on his side. Let's just close this aside by saying it is far better to spend time with friends who love you than with a crush who could not care less if you were around or not.

While friendships have different guidelines unique to their socio-cultural-historical moment, and our modern understanding of what constitutes a friendship is mostly incompatible with Jesus' ultimate example, we can learn a lot from the New Testament. Scratch that. We *have* a lot to learn. In an article on the theme of Friendship in John's Gospel, O'Day writes, "[F]riendship is one of the ways in which the revelation of God in Jesus is extended beyond the work of Jesus to the work of the disciples." She continues,

> Interestingly, the title "friend" is never used to describe Jesus in the Fourth Gospel. Throughout this gospel, Jesus has been the incarnation of

friendship without the explicit appellation. However, in speaking of his disciples' future lives, Jesus makes the explicit connection between his life of love and the conduct of friends. Jesus calls the disciples his "friends" (philoi), if they enact his commandment (15:14)—to love one another as Jesus has loved them (v. 12), to lay down their lives for their friends (v. 13). Jesus' gift of his life for others embodies friendship's highest attribute and defines the meaning and extent of "love." The title "friend" becomes something into which Jesus invites his disciples to grow. The name "friend," and with it the relationship of friendship, is a gift from Jesus to them, just as his life is a gift to them. The disciples begin with the explicit appellation, "friend," and the challenge for them is to enact and embody friendship as Jesus has done. The disciples know how Jesus has been a friend, and they are called to see what kind of friends they can become. Jesus' friendship is the model of friendship for the disciples, and it makes any subsequent acts of friendship by them possible because the disciples themselves are already the recipients of Jesus' acts of friendship.[4]

I have heard Jesus referred to as 'my friend' in various church circles, however I doubt they were thinking of the description that O'Day developed through studying the theological concept of friendship in John's Gospel. The common church meaning for calling Jesus 'friend' is used to bring him down to our level as a companion for life, someone to be open with about everyday needs and issues and make him less intimidating to modern seekers of spirituality. 'My friend Jesus' is a cool guy who is welcome at parties, doesn't mind anyone getting drunk or high or sleeping around or chasing wealth and popularity, and certainly will not bring up any sinful behavior or moral codes.

Jesus is my friend, without a question. However, our understanding of friendship needs to be reframed by the Gospel so that we do not continue to lose sight of what that meant in its original context. To return to O'Day, like the disciples who did everyday life and intimately knew how Jesus had been a friend, we are all called to see what kind of friends we can become, with Jesus as our example. We might call Jesus our friend, but unless we lay down our life for him, and for the friends around us, according to the example he gave us, *he will not call us his friends.* John 15:14 has a clause. Jesus freely gives the offer of friendship; however, we are not recognized as friends of Jesus without obedience to his commandments. Rest assured, I am not proposing that works-salvation is a valid biblical soteriology or is a component of friendship. Jesus was not qualifying how to be saved but how to be known as his friend.

There are not many commandments to point to either. "My command is this: Love each other as I have loved you" (John 15:12). Jesus makes it simple. He even solidifies it by repeating the command in 15:17. Yet a life of sacrificial love, i.e. the way that Jesus loved the disciples, is a constant journey and struggle. It is hard enough with family, where we have obligations through blood, but laying down your life for all your friends is part of this too.

Having a more holistic and robust theology of biblical friendship will form and prepare us far more for a fulfilling life, and even marriage, than the shallow social contract that society promotes. A friend can, and among followers of Jesus should, be more than just someone who is fun to hang out with, someone who shares certain interests or viewpoints, someone who makes an evening a bit less lonely. These are good aspects to be enjoyed within friendship. However, Jesus was so much than that as a friend and he calls his apprentices to live as he did.

It is also critical to understand friendship as the cornerstone of any good marriage yet without the catch that a deep friendship *must* lead to marriage. Here, a caution is in order. There is a level of intimacy between men and women that quickly becomes unhealthy when there are differing opinions about where the friendship is headed. Different people will have varying boundaries when it comes to vulnerable sharing with their circle of friends, however, constant exploration of the deep levels of self will bond individuals heart-to-heart. The trust and security required to foster these conversations often brings romantic feelings on board and, without constant communication of intention, it is easy to slip into a dating-style relationship without the commitment. At this point, it is inevitable that the person with the stronger feelings will get hurt, unless of course the friendship is taken to the next level.

I have had many dear guy friends and I highly recommend having adventures and casual one-on-one interactions, like coffee catchups, to appreciate the variety of humanity that you discover in the opposite genetic gender. With all these men, there was a line that we simply did not cross; many such topics were fair game with my female friends and never felt like unwanted intimacy. However, there were a couple of exceptions to this rule about the depth explored with a man: one slid into the territory of an emotional affair and the other ended in heartbreak. Both times I had let my guard down, had built trust, and had entangled my heart with dreams for the future. Both times the men were initiating and inviting intimacy, yet they did not pursue a committed relationship.

We cannot guard our hearts from all pain due to unbalanced expectations. C. S. Lewis said it well:

> To love at all is to be vulnerable. Love anything
> and your heart will be wrung and possibly broken.
> If you want to make sure of keeping it intact

you must give it to no one, not even an animal. Wrap it carefully round with hobbies and little luxuries; avoid all entanglements. Lock it up safe in the casket or coffin of your selfishness. But in that casket, safe, dark, motionless, airless, it will change. It will not be broken; it will become unbreakable, impenetrable, irredeemable. To love is to be vulnerable.[5]

We can be vulnerable and love our friends well. Yet, we must also exercise caution and wisdom in our romantically-intrigued friendships. Have courageous conversations about feelings and expectations, while also doing the internal work to guard your heart. Be ready to forgive. Keep short accounts. And delight in getting the privilege of seeing people more clearly as you grow in understanding who they are.

I can honestly say for myself that the courage to be vulnerable and develop deep friendships, even with the man who broke my heart, was well worth it. Community without masks is truly meaningful and gives us space in our singleness to discover how to be the sort of friend that Jesus talks about. It also reminds us that we are not alone in our journey and struggles, that many of the issues we fight in singleness are just as prevalent in marriages, and that as we bear each other's burdens we grow. Contentment, resiliency, and empathy are all character traits that grow out of becoming a true friend.

Developing deep friendships requires a solid commitment to prioritizing humans. It means a willingness to put aside your preconceptions of friendship and discover the way that Jesus demonstrated for us. At times it will hurt; vulnerable people are seen as easy targets or door mats. Yet, the mature disciple discovers that becoming like Jesus means giving up our right to be taken advantage of. Richard Foster discusses both submission and service as separate spiritual disciplines. Both are radically necessary for true community.

On submission, he writes:

> Power is discovered in submission. The foremost symbol of this radical servanthood is the cross. "He [Jesus] humbled himself and became obedient unto death, even death on a cross" (Phil. 2:8). But note this: Christ not only died a "cross-death," he lived a "cross-life." The way of the cross, the way of a suffering servant was essential to his ministry. Jesus lived the cross-life in submission to all human beings... The cross-life of Jesus undermined all social orders based on power and self-interest. [6]

And then on service:

> Self-righteous service fractures community. In the final analysis, once all the religious trappings are removed, it centers in the glorification of the individual. Therefore it puts others into its debt and becomes one of the most subtle and destructive forms of manipulation known. True service builds community. It quietly and unpretentiously goes about caring for the needs of others. It draws, binds, heals, builds.[7]

> Right here we must see the difference between choosing to serve and choosing to be a servant. When we choose to serve, we are still in charge. We decide whom we will serve and when we will serve. And if we are in charge, we will worry a

great deal about anyone stepping on us, that is, taking charge over us.

But when we choose to be a servant, we give up the right to be in charge. There is great freedom in this. If we voluntarily choose to be taken advantage of, then we cannot be manipulated. When we choose to be a servant, we surrender the right to decide who and when we will serve. We become available and vulnerable.[8]

It is the union of submission and service that trains us to be the friends of Jesus. These two disciplines form the essence of what it looks like to die to self-interest and love others in the way that Jesus commanded us. And I suspect that communities of such friends will be the most culturally subversive form of fulfilling relationships possible, not to mention the best training ground for a healthy marriage.

We all certainly dream of loyal, unselfish, available, non-manipulative, submissive, life-giving relationships. Let us make the decision today to be such friends and make the changes in our lives to prioritize people. Jesus did not wait for anyone else to take initiative. Neither should we.

Practice

Before you flip the page and keep reading, take a moment to sit quietly with the Lord and ask a few questions:

1. What thoughts, sentences, or concepts resonated with you? Which ones irritated you? What ideas did you immediately want to reject? Your visceral, emotional responses are teachers of truth that your body knows, and your mind may not be willing to process. Don't run from

the visceral response; pain is an indication that healing is needed.

2. Based on the above exercise, are there memories or emotions that you need to process? How have you understood friendship?

3. Brainstorm ways to become a more biblical friend. Are there people that you need to make more of an effort to connect with?

4. What step is God inviting you to take because of this exercise?

THANKFUL NOT BITTER

I can remember it all too clearly. A mere two months after my heartbreak, I was sitting in a white, wooden chair while a dear friend walked down the aisle, in her perfectly fitted white dress, to marry a wonderful and godly man. As happy as I was for them, it was not my first emotion. The first feeling that bubbled up was a pang of bitterness attended by a thought that ran along the lines of "why does God give all my friends their dream partner, and I'm the collector of rejection?"

Obviously, I did not want to carry that deep bitterness with me through the wedding celebration, yet it was so hard to shake. Especially because of my recent heartbreak, though that is no excuse, I felt the sting of rejection, the bite of not being wanted by a man, more than I usually did while attending a wedding. It was painfully hard to escape from the clutches of bitterness and celebrate my friends' new loving union when the deepest dream of my heart was so beyond any foreseeable fulfillment that it may as well have been decimated by an atomic bomb.

I also clearly remember the first time I fell into a gorse bush. I was hiking along the shore of Mākara, a stunning and wild section of coastline close to Wellington, NZ. The rocky beach runs straight into steep hills, and I had determined to try to climb one for a specific photo angle, only to trip and fall hands-first into a patch of gorse.

For those who don't know, gorse is a gorgeous shrub with thin, dusty green branches and vibrant yellow blossoms reminiscent of dragon snaps. All of which is amazing and delightful to the eyes; I loved my introduction to gorse bushes in Scotland when I captured them with the click of a DSLR. However, those thin branches are densely covered in scalpel-sharp spikes. The thorns can penetrate basically any fabric; though I never went tramping in ballistic nylon or Kevlar, which I assume would be safe, anything that worked as protection against blackberries or wild Alberta roses in the Rocky Mountains was useless when confronted with gorse.

Obviously, bare skin is extra susceptible to those thorns. I had a handful in my palm that stuck around to irritate and aggravate for well over two weeks past the incident. Eventually my body pushed the gorse thorns free, while I did anything I could to pry them out.

These two stories are entirely unrelated except for an allegorical link which I've become fond of: bitterness is the gorse bush of the heart.

Not only are gorse bushes dangerous to walk into, but they spread like weeds and are incredibly difficult to remove once they begin to sprout up. Your best bet is to get them out, roots and all, while they are still young plants. Otherwise, they develop into impenetrable strands, propagating more if set ablaze, and their seeds can remain viable in the earth for up to three decades. Once you have a gorse infestation, you are hard pressed to remove it.[1]

Again, bitterness is the gorse bush of the heart. Once bitterness starts to sprout up it quickly propagates, getting more and more entrenched, and lays down seeds that will hang around for decades just waiting to spring into action. It's no wonder that the Bible tells us to uproot it from our heart (Eph 4:31-32).

I dream of becoming the sort of person who can freely celebrate the love and partnership of others without the bitter wondering why my desire is still unmet. Some days, when I've been consistent with the heart-work to join the Holy Spirit in weeding out bitterness, I have no issue doing this. However, I am not yet consistent. I still have days where I hear about a new relationship forming, an engagement, or even a baby announcement, and my first reaction is "God, why not for me?"

Bitterness is an iteration of pride feeding off comparison and frustration. It stems from pride because it refuses to admit that the choice between good and bad is not ultimately up to us. Pride allows us to be angry that the thing that we believe is good should also be ours when we want it, and since we do not currently have it, it is not good timing; we have been wronged. This angry pride stares intently at the lives of others and deeply desires what they have, to the point of obsession. It refuses to be grateful for the limitations and gifts of the current season. And the mingling of these emotions with the frustration that comes with feeling left out, overlooked, or left behind by the stories of others, becomes the cocktail that is bitterness. It is a poisonous drink down to the last dregs.

The first sip feels good; acknowledging that a dream is held and not fulfilled is healthy. But to continue to drink the draught that bitterness offers is to drown the initial expression of pain with a numbing agent that refuses to take responsibility to respond to life as it is. For bitterness cannot rejoice in the good things of life; it is blind to them by choice.

The interconnected nature of bitterness and anger is worth exploring. Anger embraced leads to bitterness; without initial anger, there can be no bitterness. Weaving psychology and theology together, Dallas Willard exposes the exponential danger of anger when cocooned in the human heart:

> The answer to this question of why people embrace anger and cultivate it is one we must not miss if we are to understand the ways of the human heart. Anger indulged, instead of simply waved off, always has in it an element

of self-righteousness and vanity. Find a person who has embraced anger, and you find a person with a wounded ego...Anger embraced is, accordingly, inherently disintegrative of human personality and life. It does not have to be specifically "acted out" to poison the world. Because of what it is, and the way it seizes upon the body and its environment just by being there, it cannot be hidden. All our mental and emotional resources are marshaled to nurture and tend the anger, and our body throbs with it. Energy is dedicated to keeping the anger alive: we constantly remind ourselves of how wrongly we have been treated. And when it is allowed to govern our actions, of course, its evil is quickly multiplied in heartrending consequences and in the replication of anger and rage in the hearts and bodies of everyone it touches.[2]

Bitterness develops from the wounded ego. Within the context of singleness, it blames others for not choosing you, whether romantic or platonic interests are at play. It focuses on the good fortune of the friends around you who are living in your dreams and secretly despises them through the lens of envy; if you had their partner, you would not complain as they do, or treat them with contempt, or take them for granted, or, or, or. Like anger, bitterness does not just affect your inner world. It spreads out and impacts everyone you encounter.

Bitterness is the gorse bush of the heart. It seems inviting, with those indulgent flowers, but anyone who gets close will be stabbed; it is inevitable. And when you have drained the cup of poison, your wounded ego will establish deep roots that spread from one area of your life to another. It is unlikely that bitterness in romance will not leech over to the realm of work, family, hobbies, and beyond. There is no way to limit its spread of vindictive frustration and ingratitude without doing the deep work to reframe your disappointment, forgive those involved, and let go of the self-righteous anger.

Disappointment during the season of singleness is unavoidable, the timing of dreams being fulfilled is out of our hands, but bitterness is optional. Only you can decide whether you will approach singleness with gratitude or bitterness. No one else can make the choice for you.

Refusing to process the facets of your wounded ego will only prolong your season of singleness. Have you ever met a bitter person and felt drawn to continue to spend increasing amounts of time with them? The answer is unlikely to be yes, though there are individuals who have either a high capacity to endure the company of bitter friends or have the drive to fix them and will devote a lot of energy to this cause.

Or, to put it even more bluntly, is bitterness a quality you would desire in a spouse?

Certainly not!

It is amazing that we would wonder at our singleness if we have deep, undealt with bitterness constantly stabbing those around us. Lysa Terkeurst gives bitterness a whole chapter in her book *Forgiving What You Can't Forget*; she drives the point home "All bitterness is corrosive. It eats away at our peace. And most of us aren't making the connection that the heaviness and unsettledness that ebbs and flows in our lives is evidence of unforgiveness."[3]

Bitterness reminds us that there is work to be done in our heart posture towards others. It is testimony to a felt wrong which we are nursing and clinging to rather than releasing. Later in her book, Terkeurst states, "Confession breaks the cycle of chaos inside of me. Forgiveness breaks the cycle of chaos between us."[4] In order to back off from bitterness, we must first acknowledge the pain. The wound must be brought forward into the light so it can be dealt with and in the same moment, bitterness must be named for what it is. Even simply confessing bitterness is a step towards healing; this breaks the hold of shame.

Yet, you cannot simply confess bitterness. That is merely pointing to the gorse bush that has overtaken your heart. You have to forgive, and, in doing so, give permission to the Holy Spirit to uproot the brambles of bitterness. This is what the writer of Hebrews is reminding us of when they pair peaceful relationships with avoiding bitterness. "Make every effort to live in peace with everyone and to be holy; without holiness no one will see the Lord. See to it that no one falls short of the grace of God and that no bitter root grows up to cause trouble and defile many" (12:14-15).

One of the lesser talked about definitions of holiness is uniqueness. Bitter people are as common as the sand on the seashore; someone who lives a life of forgiveness, in peace with those around them, and without bitterness, is as uncommon as finding a freshwater pearl in the middle of the desert. Choose to be a person who walks in forgiveness and thereby peace. Be unique because bitterness does not have a strong root in your heart. Not only will it benefit your relationships with others, but it will draw you closer to the Lord.

Deep in Tolkien's lore, there is a story about Melko and Ungoliont darkening the light of Valinor. An evil spirit in the form of an unlovely spider, Ungoliont has an insatiable thirst to consume light, yet she emits thick darkness. The gloom of her presence covers their approach to the trees of Valinor; Silpion is the source of silver moonlight and Laurelin gives the golden sunlight. Melko attacks the roots of Laurelin so that Ungoliont can drink the great light; even after sucking the golden tree dry, she is not satisfied. She must have the silver moonlight as well. However, they are attacked by an elf, and in the fray, the poison of the great spider gets into the roots of Silpion; "it dried the very sap and essence of the tree, and its light died suddenly to a dismal glow lost in impenetrable dusk."[5]

My inner geek is now thoroughly indulged and has drawn a parallel to the insatiable nature of bitterness and how it spreads. If you're not vibing with my gorse bush imagery, you can now imagine bitterness as a giant, hideous spider, just waiting to suck the light from your life and poison the light for others. Unforgiveness and the wounded ego nurture this spider, lurking in the dark places of your heart, and when it does crawl out, one spindly leg at a time, it does so to destroy. It will bite and claw and consume the delight of others. If left to fester, as Ungoliont was, beware of the brood that bitterness gives birth to! Shelob, of *Lord of the Rings* fame, was a child of Ungoliont and she could not even look upon light.

Kill the spider! Do it while it is young and easy to catch. Slay bitterness with forgiveness, releasing the wounds done to your ego and the need for others to validate them. Uproot the spreading gorse bush, which is probably home to a handful of spiders anyways and destroy every spine and bramble. Roots and all. You do not need an apology to choose forgiveness. Nor do you need another's awareness of your inner turmoil to begin to deal with your wounded ego. Jesus sees it all and he wants to set you free from it.

He has done so for me, many times and counting.

A recent wedding I attended was for dear friends in Wellington, New Zealand. I can honestly say there was not a shred of bitterness present. No self-pity assailed me while I was reclining on the red leather seat with an empty spot next to me, the plus-one having become a plus-none. Mingling with drinks and dancing the night away, I was simply there to celebrate the official union of two beloved friends and to support them as the next chapter of their lives begins together. I had spent the month prior intentionally grieving a dream being shredded; it was careful work to root out the bitterness that had sprung up alongside romantic rejection. Yet, it has been integrated into my process of letting go, right at the start. I am determined to allow the Holy Spirit to remove all traces of bitterness from my life.

Anyways, if Shelob had shown up, there were plenty of swords on hand to deal with the attack. My newlywed friends are likewise LoTR fans and had replica swords in the reception hall.

Now for something that feels different but is entirely interrelated. Gratitude.

Oh, my friends, gratitude is the antidote to the poison of bitterness. Something shifts in our being when we choose to be thankful rather than dwelling on our frustration. There is a reason that Paul talks so much about being thankful, even writing such directives from prison. Here are a handful of examples; "always giving thanks to God the Father for everything, in the name of our Lord Jesus Christ" (Eph 5:20); "strengthened in the faith as you were taught, and overflowing with thankfulness" (Col 2:7); "And whatever you do, whether in word or deed, do it all in the name of the Lord Jesus, giving thanks to God the Father through him" (Col 3:17); "Devote yourselves to prayer, being watchful and thankful" (Col 4:2); "Rejoice always, pray continually, give thanks in all circumstances, for this is God's will for you in Christ Jesus" (1 Thess 5:16-18).

Often, Paul links prayer, rejoicing and thankfulness together. This triune collaboration takes our focus off the situation at hand and redirects it to God. It is not a band-aid, or at least in best practice this is not the case, but rather something of a spiritual step ladder. The order of the rungs is not always the case of every situation, but loosely, prayer is the first step, followed by rejoicing and thankfulness. At first glance, rejoicing and thanksgiving may seem like the same thing. However, to rejoice is to be glad, be well and thrive, whereas thanksgiving is to express gratitude. The first is the choice of an emotional state and the second is the choice of gracious reception.

Prayer is the conscious turning of your mind from what is happening, around or to you, and giving God your attention instead. This gives space for expressing your immediate reactions; you do not need a filter. Just read through the Psalms, the prayer book of Israel, and see that this is true. You do not need to protect God from your unsavory human emotions. He is already aware of them. To sanitize your prayers is to lie to God, to dishonor him, to mistrust his nature. Remember that Jesus expressed anger, grief, joy, surprise, and so forth. It is no surprise to God that you feel angry when your ego is wounded and your will is thwarted; he feels the same about human disobedience, only there is no sin to corrupt his emotions.

As Peter reminds us, "cast all your anxiety on Him because He cares for you" (1 Peter 5:7). Engagement in prayer is simply a method of communication. Talking to God and casting your anxiety to him recognizes that he is beyond your feelings about the situation. He cares for you, longing to receive your anger, hurt, sorrow, anxiety, and so forth, and to carry it so that you are not driven to bitterness because of it. The relief that comes from the lifting of your cares naturally blossoms into thanksgiving. This too is part of the order of creation, one of the natural laws.

Just think of the appreciation that spontaneously bubbles up when you have too many things in your hands and someone either opens the door for you or helps you with your load. You do not have to remind yourself to feel thankful in that moment because of the relief that comes from no longer struggling on your own.

As humans corrupted by the fall, we must learn again each day to trust God. This is why, when we do not give him our anxieties and cares, whether emotional, physical, or spiritual, we do not trust him. Whether it is because of a father wound that has convinced you that your Father in the Heavens could not possibly care about your thoughts; because of broken trust in a partnership that has made you suspicious of anyone attempting to share the duties of life; because of pride that has grown a fierce independence which sees help as undesired pity; there are myriad reasons why we do not see God as caring or able to help us. But the truth is, he is more than able to do so. The practice of casting your cares upon him and the peace that follows will grow both your ability to trust him and to respond in gratitude.

The more you find reasons to be grateful, the more difficult you will find it to be bitter. A heart of curated anger cannot co-exist with a heart of intentional gratitude. Anger wants to nurse the wounded ego and feed it with the injustices of life; gratitude seeks to let go of anger and pain because there is healing through release. The spiritual discipline of gratitude has been well documented throughout the history of the church. It is more recently finding itself supported by scientific studies. Gratitude has been linked to resiliency[6], to higher levels of mental wellbeing[7], even as an antidote to depression[8].

The root of thankfulness is simple: God has provided all that you need for today.

More specifically, gratitude sets you on the path to contentment in your singleness. As you begin to reflect on the basic areas where you can give thanks, it is a quick transition to finding specifics in your season for which you are grateful. The major gift of singleness is time; to understand singular devotion to your apprenticeship to Jesus; to work through emotional baggage which would sabotage a future relationship; to deepen your character; to freely give of your time without consulting the schedule of another; to discover your vocation and how your unique contribution builds up the body of Christ; these and many other areas are easily burdened when done with a life partner. While we may yearn for the romance we see in our married friends' lives, the truth is they often miss the freedom of time they had in their singleness. Recalling that can help you rejoice and give thanks for the opportunities you currently have plus the freedom to pursue them.

We do not choose thankfulness because everything about singleness is observably good, rather we do so because it contains many good things which are just waiting for us to observe. Take a moment to pause. You have time to read, uninterrupted by your partner asking for your help with a task you would rather not do or by children who ask you the same questions endlessly every two minutes. You can choose to put this book down and answer a call from a friend to meet spontaneously, without first confirming someone else has made plans for you. You could break open a journal and begin to work through some bitterness and emotional baggage that is holding you back and receive the healing forgiveness of the Lord in an intimate space.

It is time my friend. Time that you and I stop viewing singleness as a prison of rejection and loneliness to be endured, but rather a season that is beautiful and challenging in its own right, just as marriage also is. There is a lot to be grateful for in singleness. God's goodness and blessing on your life is no less present because you are not married. Each day brings a new portion of his mercies, overflowing faithfulness and steadfast love. May we take the time to see them and receive them with gratitude.

Practice

Before you flip the page and keep reading, take a moment to sit quietly with the Lord and ask a few questions:

1. What thoughts, sentences, or concepts resonated with you? Which ones irritated you? What ideas did you immediately want to reject? Your visceral, emotional responses are teachers of truth that your body knows, and your mind may not be willing to process. Don't run from the visceral response; pain is an indication that healing is needed.

2. Based on the above exercise, are there memories or emotions that you need to process? Are there areas of bitterness which have been exposed and now need to be dealt with?

3. Brainstorm ways to choose to be thankful and practice gratitude. Develop an early warning system for detecting the seeds of bitterness so you can destroy them before they take root.

4. What step is God inviting you to take because of this exercise?

END IDOLATRY

|||||||||||||||||||||||||||||||

I was saving up for a tattoo session. Wherever you sit on the debate, please put aside any knee-jerk reactions to quote Leviticus 19:28 or approving nods as you roll up your own sleeves. This story is here for a far different reason. That aside, while I was scraping together whatever extras I could for the tattoo fund, I was also fundraising for a trip to work for a week at Camp Yukon. I had already covered my own expenses and was assisting the team; I had even given what I thought was above and beyond, but one day God asked for more.

In fact, he asked for my tattoo savings to be given to the mission team.

I was not emotionally prepared for this request. It felt so out of the blue, so deep from the outfield that it could not possibly be God's voice. Give what he had been giving me in response to my petition? Be generous with something I had been waiting for, out of an abundance that was already accounted for? Put more money into a trip I had already paid for, beyond my own expenses? God would not ask that. Or would he?

You may be chuckling to yourself at what seems like an obvious answer in a trivial area. Nearly all humans are selfish to the core and the forces of evil are not going to tempt us to generous acts. Of course it was God asking me to give up something precious. It was not about the money or the tattoo, rather his prompting highlighted an idol in my life as if he had turned on flood lights in the middle of dark sky country.

The tattoo had become an idol. It was not about the mission's team needing a little boost, God could have gotten the money from any number of generous church donors, but it was my reaction to his request. How could God ask me to give up something he had confirmed I could have? The fact that I had any money to save while living alone in Vancouver was a miracle in and of itself. I was at peace when I booked the appointment; money had already been irreversibly deposited. Now, out the blue, God was so gently asking me to reallocate the lump sum of savings.

I fought him. Until I realized what he was up to, I was unwilling to let go. The moment it clicked in that it was not about the tattoo itself, but what the tattoo had come to mean to me, a precious indicator of personality that I felt unfulfilled without, I was abashed. It was about an idol that had taken up residence in my heart and I was not aware of it.

It was a painful realization. Repenting with tears, I reaffirmed my loyalty to Jesus, and him alone. And knowing how good I can be at talking myself out of things, I immediately released the money into the mission's account. Regret struck as the parting shot of the idol; the peace and joy of Jesus washed away any doubts I had about the sound of his voice.

Anything can become an idol. Even, or should I say especially, marriage.

Sit with me for a moment in the discomfort of that sentence. What happened to your emotional state as you read that marriage may be an idol? As I assert it again, feel the feelings.

Marriage easily becomes an idol.

Take a deep breath here. Again, allow yourself to sit with that statement. Do not rush past it but digest it slowly.

Have you allowed your dream of marriage to draw you into idolatry?

Let me be the first to raise my hand. This is an ongoing

challenge for me. And I am not hesitant or uncomfortable assuming it has been so for you.

It is often a pantheon that accompanies marriage in the idolatrous temple of our hearts; sex, romance, status, even the attractive man or woman themselves. They demand sacrifice of attention and desire, promising all the happiness of the cheesiest romantic comedies, while they slowly divert your heart away from God. Like bitterness, idolatry hands you the poisoned chalice with a seductive smile, knowing the first sip goes down unnoticed. Yet, this too is potent and addictive. It is the repetition that entices your heart to worship unworthy desires. I say unworthy not because the desires by themselves are wrong, but because they simply are not God.

To quote Gandalf, "there is only one lord of the ring...and he does not share power"[1]

Many people mistake God for Sauron; while the dark lord was the rightful master of the ring of power, he was not the rightful ruler of *Arda*. Sauron wanted all to come under his dominion because he was a power-hungry tyrant. However, God desires to be the sole object of our worship because he is truly the only possibility for deserving it. God does not command total devotion because he does not want to share our affections with other gods; rather, he commands it because he knows that those idols will destroy our lives. They lie to us and then kill, steal and destroy our hopes and dreams. On the other hand, God is life itself and he freely shares it with all who come to him. He even shares his power to rule and reign, but that is another book for another time.

Every time I look to a man to save me from my loneliness, from my singleness, I get myself in trouble. I build him up in my mind as the messiah who will end the exile of singleness and bring me to the promised land of marriage. But the Messiah has already come, and looking to anyone else will keep me in exile rather than living in the Promise, the Kingdom, here and now. All too often, I gaze at the beauty of Jesus and then grumble about his leadership, about how long it is taking him to get me to a place where the dream is fulfilled, longing to go back to the comfort of fixating on a specific man or marriage in general. Yet, that fixation is to return to the idolatrous land of Egypt, a place of slavery and bondage.

God, and God alone, is worthy of all the attention and affection that I long to give to a man in marriage.

Now, I am not saying that marriage is a bad dream. There is nothing wrong with desiring union. Marriage is a gift from God and his solution to the "not good" of Adam working alone in the garden of Eden (Gen 2:18). But when that dream surpasses my yearning for God, that is when the dream builds itself a shrine and takes up residence.

There is a tension that comes with dreams. It is simply having the courage to look towards the potential future with hope yet doing so with an open hand. We must hold our desires lightly, bringing them before God and asking him to fulfill them, yet trusting his wisdom to provide each day what we need. That may or may not include our dreams. As we grow in maturity, we begin to recognize that following our Good Shepherd means that he may lead us places we do not expect, that there will be dark valleys, and that we cannot run off in whatever direction we prefer; however, there is always plenty of provision for today.

If each day passes and I am still single, I trust that is good. Because I trust that God is good.

History tells us about a general who destroyed his boats as a radical declaration that there was no turning back. Hernán Cortés was a Spanish Conquistador. In 1519, he led a force to Mexico. He won his men through his charisma, yet he trained them into a unified force through exercise and discipline. "But the ultimate expression of his determination to deal with disaffection occurred when he sank his ships. By that single action he committed himself and his entire force to survival by conquest."[2] By 1521, battling both the Aztecs and envious generals from his own country seeking to depose him, Cortés conquered the Aztec empire.

I too have had moments where God called me to "burn my boats". Sometimes there is a step of obedience that requires a symbolic act to mark it; at least, I find that a visual and/or physical practice helps. This is biblically grounded. We see this in the memorial stones taken from the Jordan river after Joshua led the Israelites across (Jos. 4:1-7). The purpose of the pile of stones was to give opportunity to the community to remember God's faithfulness, to retell the miracle crossing to the next generation, and to be a visual testimony to mark a turning point in the story of Israel. They went from being a nomadic tribe, wandering in the desert for forty years until the disobedient generation died off, to entering the Promised Land where they would have to fight for their permanent homes. They needed to remember and be reminded. The pile of stones stood as a witness to their radical faith, trusting that the Jordan would be subdued for them to cross, and marking the transition in their history. The stones declared: from this day forward, everything will be different.

As God helps you to topple the idols in your life, it may be helpful to mark the moment in some way. It may also require a radical change in habit, in interactions, maybe deleting a social media app or phone number. You know where your idols stand. It is time to throw them to the ground and keep your eyes fixed on Jesus.

Do not make the mistake of halfhearted obedience, like so many of Israel's kings. Jehoram, Joash, and Amaziah are all kings of Judah who personally walked well with the Lord, yet they did not lead the people into wholehearted worship. They allowed high places and the altars of idols to remain in operation, continuing to lead the people astray, while they themselves were devoted to worship at the House of God. These kings were compared to their father's righteousness, "not like David" (2 Kings 14:3). King David was known as a man after God's own heart: regardless of his moral failings, he repented and led the people to do likewise. Learn from his example and burn the shrines in your heart.

Not many of us are dealing with physical replications of animals, people or symbols to stand in place of our gods; most of our idols are more insidious than an object with demonic heritage. They require a different tactic than simply destroying a physical location or representation. Practically speaking, several steps are helpful in ending your heart idolatry. Keep in mind that these are not necessarily sequential; it just makes for easier organization.

You need to recognize the idol. This will involve the work of the Holy Spirit. Pay attention to emotional knee-jerk reactions to invitations, either through your prayer life or conversations with others, to give up something, someone, an activity or a dream. A deep, negative reaction that happens without consideration is a key notification that there is an idol being uncovered in that area.

You need to dethrone the idol. Repentance is not just asking for forgiveness but is an active turning back to Jesus and his way. Name the idol, confess your preference of it over God, and ask for his forgiveness and then for his strength and discernment in moving forward. The idol will have taken up residence in your habits. Simply trying to remove it through recognition and asking for forgiveness is not a truly repentant move; a toxic habit needs a healthy habit to fill the vacuum it leaves behind. Dr Caroline Leaf gives us insight into this process from a cognitive neuroscientific viewpoint:

> Indeed, overcoming a bad habit or addiction is not about making something go away or stop. It is about learning how to be free of the urges to act or think in a certain way, separating yourself from them and observing these desires as an experience, not a necessity...Overcoming bad habits and addictions means shifting your mental energy away from the thoughts behind

these habits—they are slowly dying, even though
they may still affect your behavior in some way.
The key point is that the habit or addiction no
longer owns you. Breaking a bad habit is not about
elimination, it is about shifting your energy away
from the habit. Where your mind goes, your brain
and body follows!... When it comes to breaking
a bad habit, if you just focus on your willpower,
you keep giving the bad habit mental energy by
thinking about it constantly, and it stays alive.[3]

Just seeing that the idol is there will not change the habits you
have wired into your brain and body through your mental energy.
The Holy Spirit is actively at work in helping you through this
process; you are not alone as you move forwards towards him.
Yet remember the passive kings who did not destroy the shrines
and high places. They were unable to break the idolatrous habits,
following the Lord with most of their heart rather than all, and
they missed out on true freedom for themselves and the people
who were under their leadership. Giving yourself a new habit of
turning to Jesus when you are tempted to give your heart to the
recognized idol can come in many forms. It will also take time;
at least sixty-three days of practice is needed to reconceptualize a
mental habit.[4] Yet, you will discover new freedom and delight in
the goodness of God.

You need to keep watch for the idol. Certain idols have a way
of sneaking back in through various doorways. Sometimes this is
because you have created a pantheon of idolatry under one roof
and each one needs to be dealt with individually. Other times, it is
because the replacement habit is another form of worshiping the
idol you were trying to dethrone. Just look at how frequently Israel
returned to worshiping the gods of the nations around them; Baal
and Asherah continue to appear throughout the Hebrew narrative.
It is when you are comfortable in your assumed security that you

need to be most vigilant. Becoming complacent in the spiritual warfare of following Jesus is a surefire way to relapse in idolatry.

Recognize, dethrone, repent, and keep watch.

To truly end idolatry, you need to do your part. In the general course of how God interacts with humanity, he does not overwrite your habits; obviously, I use "general" intentionally here, as there are plenty of stories where God broke through and freed people from various addictions, such as alcoholism or pornography, in an instant. It is simply not the norm. However, the Spirit will be at work with you, doing more behind the scenes than your obedience to repent and remove the idols could accomplish on its own.

Cognitive neuroscience is amazing and has revealed a lot about how people can train themselves to be free from their toxic thinking, choosing and habitual acting. There are many tools that you can borrow from this realm to assist you in the process. However, they stop at picking a healthier habit and do not lead you into a life of spiritual freedom. That is why we need the Holy Spirit to be our active partner in this process. Rest assured, he is already working in you.

Recently, God asked me if I would trust him with my dream of marriage, even if he never did anything with it. I wanted to throw up. It was obvious that marriage had slipped back into a place of preference, a shrine of secrecy. Yet, in that moment, I recalled many of the ways he had been faithful up to this point in my journey. I knew I could trust him, and I desired to go deeper in that trust. So, I said yes. Once again, I released my dream of marriage to him. I marked the moment with a physical, visual reminder.

I continue to have moments of struggle with the idol of marriage. But not like I used to. God is so kind and patient with me, so much more beautiful and good than I formerly knew. I know he will be so with you.

It's time, my friend. Cut down those high places. Burn the

shrines. And find a new level of freedom and delight in Jesus, our Lord and King.

Practice

Before you flip the page and keep reading, take a moment to sit quietly with the Lord and ask a few questions:

1. What thoughts, sentences, or concepts resonated with you? Which ones irritated you? What ideas did you immediately want to reject? Your visceral, emotional responses are teachers of truth that your body knows, and your mind may not be willing to process. Don't run from the visceral response; pain is an indication that healing is needed.
2. Based on the above exercise, are there memories or emotions that you need to process? Did you become aware of idols that you need to cast down? Are you holding so tightly to marriage that God has no room to work in your season of singleness?
3. Brainstorm ways to worship God in every area of your life. Worship is so much more than music on a Sunday morning. As you focus on Jesus, and build your life around his way, you will discover new ways to worship him.
4. What step is God inviting you to take because of this exercise?

KINGDOM FOCUSED

||||||||||||||||||||||||||||||||

Now the narrative introduction comes to a grinding halt. I do not have a clever illustration or quirky life event for seeking the Kingdom, mostly because it has long been a space of Christianese and confusion. And, true to form, I have therefore spent a solid chunk of time reading and seeking and praying and digging. After all, the Kingdom was the focus of Jesus' recorded life and teachings. I reckon he cares a great deal about the topic; he also grieves for our misunderstanding and misalignment of the Kingdom vision.

This chapter could be an entire book. In fact, Dallas Willard has a rich, dense discourse which has helped me shape a deeper understanding of the Kingdom; there will certainly be many quotes here, but I recommend that you read *The Divine Conspiracy: Rediscovering Our Hidden Life in God*.

All that being said, as Jesus was focused on teaching the Kingdom of Heaven, I would be sorely remiss if I did not attempt this chapter from the perspective of singleness. Our teacher, Jesus, was single and celibate himself. He modeled a full and rich life without sex, marriage, or children, focused on doing only what the Father showed him (John 5:19). However, as Dr. Richard Hayes reminded me, Jesus had a mission and mandate different from the Genesis command to be fruitful and multiply. The life of Paul, or more modern individuals such as Luci Swindoll, is perhaps a better practical example. Singleness and marriage are equally preparation phases for becoming people who can freely live under the just, right, and loving rule and reign of Jesus Christ in the Kingdom, now and not yet.

If we sat down for a cup of coffee and a chat and I asked you how you would explain the Kingdom of Heaven, what would you say?

Maybe you would align with a quick Google search showing a vague answer about the realm where God's will is done. Or you would assume it has to do with eschatology and the end of the world. You might even look confused and ask why I want to talk about a movie from 2005 with Orlando Bloom and Liam Neeson. And you might not have any answer at all, other than knowing Jesus mentioned it once or twice.

Whether I guessed your answer or was so far off base, this is an important question. It will radically shape your season of singleness or have no impact at all. When you start to catch Jesus' vision of the Kingdom, you cannot help but want in; it is one of the reasons so many people flocked to see him and then followed him around.

Let's try a few scholars.

N. T. Wright: "'Kingdom of God' was not a vague phrase, or a cipher with a general religious aura. It had nothing much, at least in the first instance, to do with what happened to human beings after they died. The reverent periphrasis 'kingdom of heaven', so long misunderstood by some Christians to mean 'a place, namely heaven, where saved souls go to live after death', meant nothing of the sort in Jesus' world: it was simply a Jewish way of talking about Israel's God becoming king. And when this god became king, the whole world, the world of space and time, would at last be put to rights."[1]

Tim Mackey: "So Isaiah 52 then says, "Yahweh salvation came. Not only did no one believe it, but people rejected the very king who came to bring the message." And then it's the sufferings servant of Isaiah 53. So these chapters I think were crucial for Jesus' self-understanding and understanding his vocation, and what it meant for him to bring the kingdom. Because how would Jesus be exalted as king and what kind of Kingdom did he see himself bringing? So, all of this, God's going to come personally and return to his people as King. He's going to form a new people, liberate them, confront evil, and then invite them to live under his reign."[2]

Dallas Willard: "Mark's Gospel reports that "Jesus then came into Galilee announcing the good news from God. 'All the preliminaries have been taken care of,' he said. 'and the rule of God is now accessible to everyone. Review your plans for living and base your life on this remarkable new opportunity'" (Mark 1:15). In Matthew's account of Jesus' deeds and words, the formulation repeatedly used is well-known "Repent, for the kingdom of the heavens is at hand" (3:2; 4:17; 10:7). This is a call for us to reconsider how we have been approaching our life, in light of the fact that we now, in the presence of Jesus, have the option of living within the surrounding movements of God's eternal purposes, of taking our life into his life...Now God's own 'kingdom,' or 'rule,' is the range of his effective will, where what he wants done is done. The person of God himself and the action of his will are the organizing principles of his kingdom, but everything that obeys those principles, whether by nature or by choice, is *within* his kingdom."[3]

Darrell Johnson: "In using the term 'kingdom of God,' the Hebrew writers of Scripture were not thinking of a place over which God would rule, nor even of an identifiable people over whom God would rule. Rather, 'kingdom of God' or 'kingdom of heaven' is a way of saying 'God is acting as King.' The kingdom of God refers to the dynamic reality of God acting as the King."[4]

I gave big block quotes for a reason. We are all trying to sort this thing out and it usually takes more than a brief sentence to get to a place of clarity. Hopefully, you are starting to get a better idea; yet my prayer is that as you finish this chapter, you will be worshiping God for his goodness in inviting you into Kingdom living.

Here is my own stab at it: the Kingdom is where the loving, just, and right rule of Jesus is actively lived out into the world through the agency of those who call him Lord, thereby doing God's good, pleasing, and perfect will to restore relationships with him, fellow humans, and creation.

Take a deep breath and sit with all of that for a moment. How does it land with you? Do you need to reconceptualize what the Kingdom means and start living as though it can be present through your own life? I am right there with you, my friend. This has been a journey for me, so I do not expect you to change your mind instantly. However, this concept, lived out by the first disciples of Jesus, is why the church expanded so radically; people engaged fully with the teachings of Jesus in their day-to-day lives and it was entirely counterculture.

Our culture needs us to wake up and live each day as apprentices of Jesus. His mandate was to teach the Kingdom culture, to invite others to do the same, and to make it real through his very life; the Kingdom was not a vague concept to Jesus. We cannot afford it to continue to have so little impact on our lives in this Western, post-modern, hedonistic, tribalistic, self-actualization-obsessed culture. How else will awakening happen in the anti-way-of-Jesus world around us, if not through revival of Kingdom culture flowing from the lives of his apprentices? I honestly believe that it will only come if we take Jesus at his word and start to actively live by his teaching. There are too many well-meaning Christians who pray for revival, yet their lives look exactly the same as their agnostic neighbors'. Revival is for those within the church; awakening is when the goodness of Christ-like culture draws those outside the church within it.

The Kingdom is central to the teaching of Jesus. His purpose is for it to bring transformation to the individual believer and thereby the church and thereby the world. Most of us have lost the plotline. While there are some churches who do actively engage and teach, living in the Kingdom of God, they are far and few between. God's will is for it to be the norm.

Jesus went around declaring; "Repent, for the kingdom of heaven has come near" (Matt 4:17). This statement is what the gospel writers refer to as the Good News. The rule of God has come close to you, and you can freely take part in it; all you have to do is recognize that all the ways you try to be god, all the ways you try to control God, and everything you thought you knew about the good life have to be discarded. Repent. Come follow Jesus instead.

In preparation for this chapter, I read the entire sermon on the mount in one sitting, out loud. The strangest thing started happening about the time I got to fasting and prayer; I was overcome with emotion. I reckon that the Holy Spirit decided to get a bit closer and smile over my reading, because I've read these words many times. Not usually in one sitting and never out loud and alone, and never with the emotion that hit me today, yet the sermon on the Mount is familiar. While it should be, as Jesus' manifesto on Kingdom living, today was a good reminder that these words carry the breath of God. That is amazing.

Willard happens to describe my encounter well:

> God's presence is the whole story. *This interaction between us and the God who is present with us always is what the resurrection is really about.* The meaning of the resurrection isn't just that Jesus won; it's that *he is now living with us.* So how does that work? It works with words. The kingdom of God works with words. Remember, we are talking about a reality that is personal through and through. That chair you are sitting on, and all of the other things we are trained so carefully to believe are independent, are not going along

on their own. They are all subject constantly to
the will and word of God. That's faith! That's 23rd
Psalm faith![5]

I encountered God's presence through reading the words
of Jesus, recorded by those who knew him and translated into
English through the diligent work of thousands of scholars. These
words still speak deeply to the human condition. Unsurprisingly,
for the Creator of our humanness, who walked for a few decades
in a body like ours, was the one who was teaching. Jesus is a
masterful teacher.

If the Kingdom is where God's will is done, the obvious
follow-up question is: what is God's will? Far too often, we get hung
up on this, looking for specific answers to specific questions so
that we stay on the spider's thread of his acute direction. Anything
else is to fall out of the sweet spot. Except, that is not how Jesus or
the Bible deals with the will of God.

Of course, there are moments where you need a straight
answer; some life decisions have bigger impact on the direction
of your life than others. But Jesus is so much kinder, more patient,
and gracious than we give him credit for; he is not staring at
you waiting for you to make the right or wrong move, hand
ready to smack you when you step just a little out of bounds. Yes,
there are real life consequences for our decisions, but nothing is
irredeemable for good by our good Father.

What you need is discernment. This is a lifelong area of
training in wisdom and Christlikeness, and it is far more useful,
not to mention realistic, than moment-by-moment directives.
Discernment helps you decide between a good choice and the best
choice. It empowers you to say yes to things that will bring forth
the Kingdom in a physical way and say no to things that hinder
Kingdom growth. Discernment opens your eyes to see what the
Father is doing and partner with him in real time, in the small
everyday decisions as well as the momentous.

Discernment flows from character. And character is of immediate concern to God's will for your life; it is your character that brings glory to God because it is the source of your habits and actions. Your character needs training. No better training can be given than the sermon on the mount.

You are probably familiar with The Sermon. However, it is likely that you know it best as piecemeal, sections pulled out of context and preached as a standalone thought of Jesus. Take a moment to read it in full. (This book can wait, especially for the words of Jesus.) There is a logic to the way that Matthew has woven the section together. Each directive builds upon that which precedes it. Whether Jesus gave this discourse in one sitting, as the narrative shows, or it is various teaching moments that Matthew compiled, it has been placed with intention in this format. The Holy Spirit is the one who inspired the author as Matthew recalled and wrote the teachings of Jesus.

Dallas Willard clued me in to the rhetoric of Jesus' words. He outlines the Sermon as laying a foundation with the basic issues that plague the human condition, focusing on anger, contempt, and lust, before teaching on areas that can only be worked out once anger no longer has a hold on your heart. Anger is given a vivid title: "the wounded ego." There is little that the wounded ego will not do to make itself seen, make others pay, and/or try to regain control. All human depravity flows from this place of nurtured and cherished anger, however secretly it may lurk beneath other emotions.

Singleness is the perfect training ground to root out anger. How many of us carry a wounded ego for having been rejected, passed over, ignored, not chosen, and so on the list goes? How many of us believe that if we were only given a chance, we would sweep away our partner with romance, yet the days fly by and no one looks in our direction? How many of us feel envy when yet another friend is asked out by someone who happened to glimpse them across the room, and it has been years since we've gone on a date?

All of us. In one area or another, you and I need to confront our anger about being single.

Honestly, I thought I had been doing well in this arena. So much of my focus was on seeking out and uprooting bitterness that I did not even see how deeply anger was buried in my heart. It was only after three separate days of undirected fasting that the Holy Spirit had the space to bring this to the surface. I had been angry at God and angry at myself; even angry at my body, which had spilled over into contempt for my body. Here I was, believing that I was in a great, healthy space with my singleness because I was not caught in the usual cycles of bitterness, when God revealed there was a deeper layer to be dealt with.

My wounded ego needed to come to the light so it could be pruned from my life.

The healing work has begun, and by no means am I totally free from this, but the lightness of spirit that came alongside the revelation can only be described as being held by the Spirit. Jesus is so patient with me, with you. He will not force us to heal; he invites us to trust him more and cut off the things in our life that hold us back from doing so.

A wounded ego will always shy away from the hand of God. It is like a stray dog that has been beaten and turned out of the house; more than likely it will bite the next hand that reaches out, even if it does so with kindness. God always extends healing to us, and we will see this more clearly as we choose to learn to trust him.

It is my anger at God about being single that has slowed my intimacy and trust with him.

It is my anger at being single that has led me to blame my body for an inability to attract a man, which has bred an underlying contempt for how God formed me.

It is my anger at being single that has caused me to focus on men as objects with lustful intention rather than appreciating them as a fellow image bearer of God.

It is my anger at being single that has led to bitterness and envy, as well as a fierce independence that struggles to allow others to do things for me.

Is this resonating with you? Are you beginning to see where anger has deep roots in your singleness, where your wounded ego has lashed out, where God is waiting to bring deep, inner wholeness? These are crucial areas to lift to God with open hands, especially in your season of singleness; these are all venomous wounds. To ignore them is to bring poison into any prospective relationship.

And this is only the very beginning of the sermon on the Mount. Jesus goes far beyond anger, the wounded ego, for the Kingdom manifesto, but he must begin there. Modern psychology has been catching up to Jesus, discovering how resilient anger is and how it affects the whole body.[6] Anger indulged is responsible for the worst of humanity.

Jesus waits. For his life to fully flow through you, there is pruning that needs to be done. Some branches are dead, and some have borne fruit but are now overgrown and reaching; they are green and leafy, but the energy goes into the wood, not fruit. Both need to go so that your life can produce more fruit, both in quality and quantity (John 15:1-17).

"The sermon – to take it for the moment as a whole – is not a mere miscellany of ethical instruction. It cannot be generalized into a set of suggestions, or even commands, on how to be 'good'. Nor can it be turned into a guide-map for how to go to 'heaven' after death. It is rather, as it stands, a challenge to Israel to *be* Israel. We may follow the main lines of the sermon and observe in outline the effect of reading it this way, as Jesus' retelling of his contemporaries' story."[7]

Who is Israel but a "chosen people, a royal priesthood, a holy nation, God's special possession" (1 Peter 2:9)? Followers of Jesus are just as much a part of the spiritual, meta-Israel as those born through the bloodline of Jacob, son of Issac, son of Abraham, seed of the promise.

Is this starting to come together for you? God, being Love, reveals himself intimately, yet intimacy does not come without obedience. Partners to rule and reign, the way God set up Eden, do not come out of fear but love. So, throughout our spiritual history, God has chosen to work with a small contingent, so that ultimately, he may be known, delighted in, obeyed, and loved by all.

Jesus knew all this. Jesus knew that the Israel of his day had degenerated to strict rule following, not of the Torah but the Mishnah; to radical zealotism, using violence as the way to reestablish God's Kingdom; or to apathy and subservience to Rome for personal gain. Jesus revealed that his life and his teaching was the true Israel, conflicting with all the other voices in his day. And ours. If Jesus' Way is what it means to be truly human, then all other ways are wrong. All.

A thought from Willard, "When he announced that the "governance" or rule of God had become available to human beings, he was primarily referring to what *he* could do for people, God acting with him. But he was also offering to communicate this same "rule of God" to others who would receive and learn it from him. *He was himself the evidence for the truth of his announcement about the availability of God's kingdom, or governance, to ordinary human existence.*"[8]

As you and I follow the Way of Jesus, as communicated through The Sermon in particular and the New Testament in general, we show the world the reality of the Kingdom of God. We make God visible. Love is not just a concept but a living reality.

Jesus taught his disciples to "seek first the Kingdom" (Matt 6:33). This means before marriage, before career, before material possessions; basically, it is a call to be radically counterculture. As singles, it is harder to get swept up in the angst of being unmarried when your focus is on learning to walk in the community of love that Jesus calls us to.

Paul focuses on the benefits of being single: un-diverted attention to the Kingdom (1 Cor 7:32-35). This is the main gift of singleness: time. Time that is not wrapped up simply because a spouse has needs, desires, plans, commitments. Time that can be freely given to inner healing and manifesting the Kingdom through unflinching devotion to Jesus and his Way.

Seeking the Kingdom is holistic. It brings all of you through an intentional, gradual, day-by-day process, under the beautiful leadership of Jesus. In practical terms, seeking the Kingdom is spiritual formation, using disciplines that have been modeled for us by Jesus and recognized as beneficial by the church in the age since. It is reordering your life and desires around God's life and desires; the Holy Spirit empowers you and does far more work than you can imagine, yet you still need to partner in the process.

It is not a program to make you into a better prospective spouse, though this is an honest side benefit.

It is not an attempt to twist God's arm into giving you your heart's desires, the magic genie ('I rub you the right way so that you will do what I want') though those dreams may be an outcome of you becoming a safe person to handle them.

It is not becoming obsessed with rules and regulations, though your life will have more boundaries than most.

Seeking first the Kingdom is getting wrapped up in the beauty, grace, love, uniqueness, absolute goodness of Jesus, of God, of the Holy Spirit, and letting that be enough. Choosing the life of Jesus over the life that the world tells us to run after. No matter what impact it has on our singleness.

A final word from Willard as we wrap up, "It is being included in the eternal life of God that heals all wounds and allows us to stop demanding satisfaction. What really matters, of a personal nature, once it is clear that *you are included*? You have been *chosen*. *God* chooses you. This is the message of the kingdom."[9]

Let us sit still with this question together. If I believe, fully and wholeheartedly, that God has chosen me, can I choose to embrace the good life he has entrusted me with, including all the challenges of being single, for as long as this season endures?

This is the climactic question, the whole point and thesis of this book. Why is singleness a good season in its own right? Because God has chosen me and that is enough. Do not be misled and overtaken by the thought that you have therefore been chosen to be single for your whole life on earth. That may be the case and it may not be. However, I suspect if you are reading this, you still dream of marriage, as I do. Seeking first the Kingdom asks that you let go of your white-knuckled death-grip on your dream; Jesus asks you to dream bigger.

Marriage is a good dream. The Kingdom is a better one.

Practice

Before you flip the page and keep reading, take a moment to sit quietly with the Lord and ask a few questions:

1. What thoughts, sentences, or concepts resonated with you? Which ones irritated you? What ideas did you immediately want to reject? Your visceral, emotional responses are teachers of truth that your body knows, and your mind may not be willing to process. Don't run from the visceral response; pain is an indication that healing is needed.

2. Based on the above exercise, are there memories or emotions that you need to process? What do you understand "seeking the Kingdom" to mean and how has that changed through this chapter?

3. Brainstorm ways to partner with God in every element of your lifestyle. Ask him for a clearer understanding of what it means to be an apprentice of Jesus.
4. What step is God inviting you to take because of this exercise?

EPILOGUE

||||||||||||||||||||||||||||||

I had a surprising revelation during a conversation with a new friend. She was expressing her hope for a new relationship to begin during the year, which led to talking about singleness and waiting. It drew out of her a very normal protestant/charismatic Christian comment that "if there is a desire in your heart, God means to fulfill it."

I paused. "I don't believe that anymore."

This is not the part that surprised me. It was what came next. I expressed that it is not bitterness that has led me to abandon that sentiment but a change in my understanding of what our deepest desires point to. I am wrestling with the thought that all our desires are meant to lead us to Christ. Even with a holy longing like marriage, a God-given dream of human union, that hope should draw me deeper into intimacy with Jesus. After all, he is the bridegroom and we, the church, are his bride.

So, what is it in singleness that I learn about the nature of Love?

How you and I answer that question will show us what we really believe about singleness.

Am I being punished or am I developing character?

Am I invisible or have I been tucked away in a safe space?

Am I undesirable or am I settled in the conviction that God has chosen me?

I do not need to keep adding to this list; I do not have all the answers or questions. But together, we can learn, grow, encourage, support, challenge, and so forth, to steward our singleness well.

In order to embrace singleness, we need to fully submit ourselves to spiritual formation, with our sole goal being intimacy with the beautiful Triune God that we call Father.

Regarding spiritual formation, Willard writes the following:

> [T]eaching, training, and guidance must be given with reference to the other aspects of the disciples' lives: body, love and sexuality, marriage and children, success with work and jobs. The object in each case is to enable the disciple to be thankful for who they are and what they have. And much the same progression will be required: from honesty to acceptance to compassion and forgiveness and then on to thankfulness to God and the honoring of our lives in all of the aspects indicated. And when this training has been completed, Paul's words will make perfect sense: "always giving thanks for all things on behalf of our Lord Jesus Christ to God, even the Father" (Eph 5:20). And again: "I have learned how to be content whatever the circumstances...I can do all things in him who gives me strength" (Phil 4:11,13).[1]

"Honesty to acceptance to compassion and forgiveness and then on to thankfulness to God." Willard's words wrap up our wrestling well. Each chapter in this book has been designed to lead you through this progression in various areas. The intention is to help you find contentment as you wait, dream, hope, pray, grieve, express frustration, and so forth.

Our contentment, our prize, our comfort, our consolation, our lover, our leader, it is Jesus.

Seeking Solo is simply that: in my singleness, seeking Jesus, and him as the sole object of my heart. Seeking Jesus as a single individual; seeking for Jesus to be the single most important person; seeking to be whole in Christ while journeying solo. It can be phrased in a delightful combination of clever ways, but it always comes back to God.

May singleness lead you ever deeper into knowing Christ.

May you discover that true intimacy is found with him in the wilderness, that no matter how alone you feel as you wait for marriage, you are never abandoned.

May you discover the deep contentment that Paul wrote about, knowing with growing certainty that Jesus is the source of your life.

May you find joy in the boundaries of sexuality; though it is difficult to constrain your passionate desires, it is more freeing to do so.

May you delight in the fellowship of others and nurture friendships that are life-giving and life-altering, regardless of any romantic potential.

May you uproot the strands of bitterness, slaying the hideous spider that threatens to poison your heart and suck the life out of those around you.

May you throw down the idols without pity or mercy, giving your full attention and worship to God alone.

May you seek first the Kingdom and its righteousness, knowing that all things will be added to you by your gracious Father (Matt 6:33).

If you will allow it, singleness is not a burden to bear; it is a good and delightful season in its own unique way. A holy way, if you will. The closer that I draw to Jesus, the more I know this to be true. The goodness of my life is not found in my dream of marriage coming true. It is found in offering up my life to the Lord who laid down his life for me. This is true now, while I am single, and it will still be true if I am invited into a covenantal life of love with a Christlike man.

That '*if*' used to frighten me. There are still days when it does, but they are becoming further and fewer between.

God is good, my friends. Let that be the final word for your singleness.

Baby Steps: Love is... Notes

1. "G3114", "Thayer's Greek Lexicon", *Blue Letter Bible.* https://www.blueletterbible.org/lexicon/g3114/kjv/tr/0-1/
2. "G5541", "Strong's Greek Lexicon", *Blue Letter Bible.* https://www.blueletterbible.org/lexicon/g5541/kjv/tr/0-1/
3. "G2206", "Strong's Greek Lexicon", *Blue Letter Bible.* https://www.blueletterbible.org/lexicon/g2206/kjv/tr/0-1/
4. "G3947", "Strong's Greek Lexicon", *Blue Letter Bible.* https://www.blueletterbible.org/lexicon/g3947/kjv/tr/0-1/
5. "G2556", "Strong's Greek Lexicon", *Blue Letter Bible.* https://www.blueletterbible.org/lexicon/g2556/kjv/tr/0-1/
6. "G93", "Strong's Greek Lexicon", *Blue Letter Bible.* https://www.blueletterbible.org/lexicon/g93/kjv/tr/0-1/
7. "G225", "Strong's Greek Lexicon", *Blue Letter Bible.* https://www.blueletterbible.org/lexicon/g225/kjv/tr/0-1/
8. "G4722", "Strong's Greek Lexicon", *Blue Letter Bible.* https://www.blueletterbible.org/lexicon/g4722/kjv/tr/0-1/
9. "G5278", "Strong's Greek Lexicon", *Blue Letter Bible.* https://www.blueletterbible.org/lexicon/g5278/kjv/tr/0-1/
10. "G1601", "Strong's Greek Lexicon", *Blue Letter Bible.* https://www.blueletterbible.org/lexicon/g1601/kjv/tr/0-1/

Wilderness and Leaning into Solitude Notes

1. Jane Austen, *Pride and Prejudice,* (Whitehall: T. Egerton, 1813), Ch 19.
2. *The Empire Strikes Back,* directed by Irvin Kershner, (1980: Los Angeles: 20th Century Studios; 2004), DVD.
3. "H5828," *Blue Letter Bible,* https://www.blueletterbible.org/lexicon/ h5828/kjv/wlc/0-1/.
4. Ami Rokach, *The Psychological Journey to and from Loneliness: Development, Causes, and Effects of Social and Emotional Isolation,* (Cambridge: Academic Press, 2019), 8.
5. Dallas Willard, *Spirit of the Disciplines: Understanding How God Changes Lives,* (New York: Harper Collins, 1988), 56-57.
6. *New International Version.* (Grand Rapids: Zondervan, 2016).
7. "G2048," *Blue Letter Bible,* https://www.blueletterbible.org/lexicon/
8. Ruth Hayley Barton, *Invitation of Solitude and Silence: Experiencing God's Transforming Presence,* (Downers Grove: InterVarsity Press, 2004), 16.

Contentment and Constraint notes

1. Dallas Willard, *Spirit of the Disciplines: Understanding How God Changes Lives,* (New York: Harper Collins, 1988), 20.
2. John Mark Comer, *The Ruthless Elimination of Hurry,* (Colorado Springs: WaterBrook, 2019), 23.
3. Donald Hebb, *https://www.ncbi.nlm.nih.gov/pmc/articles/ PMC4006178/*
4. Stephen R. Covey, *The 7 Habits of Highly Effective People*, (New York: Simon and Schuster), 105.
5. John Mark Comer, *The Ruthless Elimination of Hurry,* (Colorado Springs: WaterBrook, 2019), 88.

Boundaries in Sexuality notes

1. Beth Allison Barr, *The Making of Biblical Womanhood: How the Subjugation of Women Became Gospel Truth,* (Grand Rapids: Brazos Press, 2021), 102-103.
2. David B. Morris, *Eros and Illness,* (Cambridge: Harvard University Press, 2017), 2-3.

3. John A. T. Robinson, *The Body: A Study in Pauline Theology*, (London: SCM Press, 1952)
4. Heike Hartung, *Embodied Narration: Illness, Death and Dying in Modern Culture*. transcript Verlag, (University of Graz, 2018), 9.
5. Paula Gooder, *Body: Biblical Spirituality for the Whole Person*, (London: SPCK, 2016), 117.
6. Mark Regenerus, *Cheap Sex: The Transformation of Men, Marriage and Monogamy*, (Oxford: Oxford University Press, 2017), 67.
7. Ibid. 27.
8. Ibid. 63.
9. Martha Kempner, "Abstinence." *The International Encyclopedia of Human Sexuality*, edited by Patricia Whelehan and Anne Bolin, 1st edition, (New York: Wiley, 2015), https://search.credoreference.com/content/entry/wileyhs/abstinence/0.
10. Caroline Leaf, *Who Switched Off Your Brain? Solving the Mystery of He Said/She Said*, (Southlake: Inprov, Ltd, 2011),180-181.
11. Ariela R. Dubler, "Immoral Purposes: Marriage and the Genus of Illicit Sex," *Yale Law Journal* 115, no. 756, (2006): 763-764.
12. Olivia Stanley, "A Personal Encounter with Purity Culture: Evangelical Christian Schooling in Aotearoa/New Zealand," *Women's Studies Journal* 34, no. 1/2, (Dec. 2020): 116–29. search.ebscohost.com/login.aspx?direct=true&AuthType=shib&db=a9h&AN=147241211&site=eds-live.

Find your Fellowship Notes

1. Genesis 2:18
2. Dilip V.Jeste et al., "Battling the Modern Behavioral Epidemic of Loneliness," *JAMA Psychiatry* 77, no. 6, (Mar. 2020), doi:10.1001/jamapsychiatry.2020.0027.
3. Peter Block, *Community: The Structure of Belonging*, (Oakland: Berrett-Koehler Publishers, 2018), 1.
4. Gail R. O'Day, "Jesus as Friend in the Gospel of John," *Interpretation: A Journal of Bible and Theology* 58, no. 2, (Apr. 2004) 144–157, doi:10.1177/002096430405800204.
5. C. S. Lewis, *The Four Loves*, (Northern Ireland: Geoffrey Bles, 1960).
6. Richard J. Foster, *Celebration of Discipline*, (New York: Harper Collins, 1998), 115-116

7. ibid 129-130.
8. ibid 132.

Thankful not Bitter Notes

1. "Gorse – Weeds Database". *Massey University,* accessed July 7, 2022, https://www.massey.ac.nz/massey/learning/colleges/college-of-sciences/clinics-and-services/weeds-database/gorse.cfm
2. Dallas Willard, *The Divine Conspiracy,* (New York: Harper One, 1997), 149-150
3. Lysa Terkeurst, *Forgiving What You Can't Forget,* (Nashville: Thomas Nelson, 2020), 191.
4. Ibid. 212.
5. J. R. R. Tolkien, *The Book of Lost Tales – Part One,* (Boston: Houghton Mifflin Company, 1984), 153.
6. Veronica Scott et al. "Gratitude: A Resilience Factor for More Securely Attached Children," *Journal of Child and Family Studies* 30, (2021): 416–430, doi.org/10.1007/s10826-020-01853-8
7. Florencio F. Portocarrero et al. "A Meta-Analytic Review of the Relationship Between Dispositional Gratitude and Well-Being," *Personality and Individual Differences* 164, (2020), doi.org/10.1016/j.paid.2020.110101
8. Nicola Petrocchi and Alessandro Couyoumdjian, "The Impact of Gratitude on Depression and Anxiety: The Mediating Role of Criticizing, Attacking, and Reassuring the Self," *Self and Identity* 15, no. 2 (2016): 191-205, doi: 10.1080/15298868.2015.1095794

End Idolatry Notes:

1. *The Lord of the Rings: The Fellowship of the Ring,* directed by Peter Jackson, (2001; Wellington, NZ: New Line Cinema, Wingnut Films, 2002), DVD.
2. Ralph Hammond Innes, "Hernán Cortés," *Encyclopedia Britannica,* May 18, (2023), https://www.britannica.com/biography/Hernan-Cortes.
3. Caroline Leaf, "How to Unwire Addiction & Toxic Habits from Our Brains, Why Focusing on "Willpower" is Ineffective and Counterproductive + Tips on How to Help Someone Without Enabling Them (with Dr.

Amy Johnson)," *Dr Leaf,* Sept 27 (2020), https://drleaf.com/blogs/news/howto-unwire-addiction-toxic-habits-from-our-brains-why-focusing-onwillpower-is-ineffective-and-counterproductive-tips-on-how-to-helpsomeone-without-enabling-them-with-dr-amy-johnson

4. Caroline Leaf. "4 Steps to Reconceptualize a Toxic Thinking Habit into a Healthy New Neural Network," *Dr Leaf,* Dec 04 (2019), https://drleaf.com/blogs/news/4-steps-to-reconceptualize-a-toxic-thinking-habit-into-a-healthy-new-neural-network

Kingdom Focused Notes:

1. N. T. Wright, *Jesus and the Victory of God* (Minneapolis: Fortress Press, 1996), 202-203

2. Tim Mackey and Jon Collins, "Co-Ruling with Jesus," *The Bible Project,* Nov 10, 2015, audio, https://bibleproject.com/podcast/kingdom-god-part-2/

3. Dallas Willard, *The Divine Conspiracy,* (New York: Harper One, 1997), 15-16, 25

4. Darrell Johnson, *Fifty-Seven Words that Change the World,* (Vancouver: Canadian Church Leaders Network, 2021), 41

5. Dallas Willard, *The Allure of Gentleness,* (New York: Harper One, 2015), 160

6. Hendricks LaVelle et al., "The Effects of Anger on the Brain and Body," *National Forum Journal of Counseling and Addiction* 2, no. 1, (2013), http://www.nationalforum.com/Electronic%20Journal%20Volumes/Hendricks,%20LaVelle%20The%20Effects%20of%20Anger%20on%20the%20Brain%20and%20Body%20NFJCA%20V2%20N1%202013.pdf

7. N. T. Wright, *Jesus and the Victory of God* (Minneapolis: Fortress Press, 1996), 288

8. Dallas Willard, *The Divine Conspiracy,* (New York: Harper One, 1997) 19

9. Ibid, 340

Epilogue Notes:

1. Dallas Willard, *The Divine Conspiracy* (New York: Harper One, 1997), 340